Yoga and Psychoanalysis

This book discusses the relevance of tracing back the course of individual development noted in psychoanalysis (regression) and in Patañjali's Yoga (*prati-prasava*).

Although Freud found diagnostic benefits in tracing the history of the patients' early childhood experiences, he also recognized the influences of the history of civilization and evolution. He also viewed the regression to earlier history in a negative light. Ernst Kris, on the other hand, saw some benefits of regression. The nature and extent of the influence of Jewish mysticism on Freud is highly controversial, and scholars have pointed out the possible influence of Kabalarian mysticism, which held that enlightenment follows from going all the way back to the origin of human beings at the beginning of the cosmos. This view has an interesting parallel in Patañjali's Yoga. This volume highlights these significant parallels in the Indian and the Western systems of knowledge in the study of human psychology and explores the need for their mutual understanding. It also examines converging trends in modern psychology to recognize the need for transcendence of ego in individuals.

This book will be of immense interest to students, teachers, researchers, and practitioners of psychology, psychoanalysis, and Yoga Psychology. It will be of great interest to psychologists, counsellors, mental health professionals, clinical psychologists, yoga enthusiasts, and those interested in transpersonal psychology.

Anand C. Paranjpe obtained his PhD at Pune University and conducted post-doctoral research at Harvard University under a Fulbright and Smith-Mundt grant. In 1967 he started teaching at Simon Fraser University in Canada, where he is currently Emeritus Professor of Psychology and Humanities. He is Fellow of Canadian Psychological Association and of the National Academy of Psychology (India).

His major publications include *Theoretical psychology: The meeting of East and West* (1984) and *Self and identity in modern psychology and Indian thought* (Plenum, 1998). He co-edited with Professors K.R. Rao and Ajit Dalal the *Handbook of Indian Psychology* (2008). His more recent publication is a book titled *Psychology in the Indian tradition* (2016; 2017) which he co-authored with Prof. K. Ramkrishna Rao as its first author. He was invited by the Indian Council of Philosophical Research as National Visiting Professor in 2010–2011 and was recognized as Distinguished Psychologist by the National Academy of Psychology (India) in 2021.

"It is a fascinating work replete with scholarship and humanity. It offers a powerful methodology to achieve the highest reaches of human nature. The book delineates an outstanding fact that to grow is to go back(!), back to the original state of being and beyond from where human life began. Evolution to the highest state of being, to a state of eternal joy, is through a process of involution.

The book deals elaborately with Freudian methodology of Regression in Psychoanalytical Therapy which releases the dormant and ailing human potential. Further, it takes up even more elaborately the discussion on Patañjali's Yoga System that takes the human through a process of involution. Contrasting Involution with Regression the author goes to show yogic involution takes us beyond the psychoanalytic regression to attain the height of being that is full of Truth, Pure Consciousness and Joy.

The Author has done a tremendous job in delineating and contrasting both Regression and Involution with great scholarship. The book is a great addition to the existing global knowledge on human growth and welfare".

– **M S Thimmappa**, *Former Professor of Psychology, Bangalore University; Former Vice Chancellor, Registrar and Professor of Psychology, Bangalore University*

"In this invaluable book, Professor Paranjpe sets Freud's and Patañjali's Yoga systems side-by-side, focusing especially on psychological regression, a key concept in each system. Alongside well-known differences, he uncovers fascinating parallels, perhaps some traceable or inspired by Freud's family heritage of Hassidic Judaism. Paranjpe's readable, nuanced, and well-balanced treatment is a boon to attempts to integrate Eastern and Western psychological insights, as well as to comparative scholarship. The volume is highly recommended for seasoned scholars and teachers as well as for students seeking insight about the relation between these two influential views of human psychology".

– **Doug Oman**, *University of California, Berkeley*

"As a Kabbalistic scholar, I found profound insights into the link between Freud, Patañjali, Yoga psychology, and ontological frameworks in Kabbalah.

Anand Paranjpe weaves together significant influences from Kabbalah, Eastern/Western psychology, the works of Patañjali and others, and delivers a sound thesis on Freud's contributions to modern psychology.

Especially interesting, are discovering the roots of Freud's inspiration from the Hasadic community, and the similarities from Kabbalah's Zoharic teachings based on the Tree of Life (Etz Chiim).

Highly recommend!"

– **Bob Waxman, PhD**, *President – Kabbalah Education Network, USA*

"I found this a compelling work.

It presents and explores the process of 'regression' as manifested in India's traditions of deep psychology. It contrasts this process with its parallel in Western psychology. Through this 'regression' lens the reader reviews the history of both Eastern and Western discoveries in psychology.

I found particularly compelling the author's exposition of regression in yoga psychology as the path that the yogi takes in deconstructing one's personal self, and thus reality itself".

– **Brian Ruppenthal**, *Resident Sādhak Ramagiri Ashram, Tomales, California*

"Yoga Psychology and Psychoanalysis have their own specific contexts and purposes beyond their superficial similarities and applications in enhancing mental health and well-being. Professor Paranjpe has just picked one pair of concepts – prati prasava and regression – to provide a comparative perspective of the two systems.

The author is already known to academicians internationally for his extensive knowledge and deep scholarship in both Western and Indian philosophical systems from his two earlier works. Once again, he has brought his rich intellectual resources and has demonstrated how we can understand and bridge Indian and modern psychological thought.

This is a work of great relevance and significance in this juncture because Yoga has become a part of popular discourse. Researchers in many fields like Clinical Psychology, Past Life Regression therapy, Indigenous Psychology, Indian psychology, Transpersonal Psychology, Spiritual psychology, and so forth can avoid many pitfalls by reading this work".

– **Kiran Kumar K. Salagame, PhD**, *Vice-President, International Transpersonal Association, USA; Fellow, Indian Association of Clinical Psychologists; Former Professor of Psychology, University of Mysore, India*

"Yoga and Psychoanalysis by Anand C. Paranjpe is a refreshing and contemporary contribution to the field of mind studies. A keen student of self and identity, Paranjpe has gone into the complex and sophisticated traditions of psychoanalysis, Yoga and mystic traditions. It will be of great help to students and scholars interested in mind, consciousness, yoga and psychoanalysis".

– **Girishwar Misra, PhD**, *Ex Vice Chancellor, Mahatma Gandhi Antarrashtriya; Hindi Vishwavidyalaya, Wardha, and Former Professor and Head, Department of Psychology, University of Delhi, Delhi, India*

"This book by Dr. Anand Paranjpe is a critical addition to the knowledge base in yoga. Anand ji brings a depth of knowledge and research to the explication of the convergences and divergences between pratiprasava and regression that lie at the heart of inner transformation. This understanding is essential for researchers and practitioners who are engaged with the field of Yoga Psychology".

– **Raghu Ananthanarayanan**, *Co-founder, Ritambhara Ashram*

"Psychiatrists, psychologists and other mental health professionals generally tend to believe that mind sciences originated in the Western hemisphere with the likes of William James and Sigmund Freud leading the development of core conceptual frameworks. Contemporary cross-cultural psychologists assume the universality of the foundational ideas in psychology and explore how cultures across the globe influence them and human behavior. In stark contrast, Professor Paranjpe describes one of the central tenets in the Indic knowledge system (prati-prasava as described in Maharshi Patañjali's Yogasutras) and compares it with the phenomenon of regression as described by Sigmund Freud. This juxtaposition and comparative analysis of prati-prasava and regression will impress upon the readers the need to understand and study different epistemological traditions contributing to the field of mind sciences".

– **Rahul Shidhaye**, *Associate Professor of Psychiatry, Pravara Institute of Medical Sciences, Loni, India, and DBT-Wellcome Trust; India Alliance Intermediate Fellow in Clinical and Public Health Research*

"With his deep knowledge of both Yoga and modern psychologies, there is no better guide than Anand Paranjpe to the commonalities and differences in the two systems. This book is a welcome and scholarly addition to the project of creating a universal psychology that is not limited by its Western origins".

– **Sudhir Kakar**, *Psychoanalyst, Author*

Yoga and Psychoanalysis

Perspectives on the Psychology of Regression

Anand C. Paranjpe

Routledge
Taylor & Francis Group
LONDON AND NEW YORK

First published 2022
by Routledge
4 Park Square, Milton Park, Abingdon, Oxon OX14 4RN

and by Routledge
605 Third Avenue, New York, NY 10158

Routledge is an imprint of the Taylor & Francis Group, an informa business

British Library Cataloguing-in-Publication Data
A catalogue record for this book is available from the British Library

Library of Congress Cataloging-in-Publication Data
A catalog record for this book has been requested

ISBN: 978-1-032-07982-0 (hbk)
ISBN: 978-1-032-24714-4 (pbk)
ISBN: 978-1-003-27986-0 (ebk)

DOI: 10.4324/9781003279860

Typeset in Times New Roman
by Apex CoVantage, LLC

Dedicated to the memories of The Late Professor Erik H. Erikson, a great teacher, and The Late Professor David Bakan, a superb mentor.

Contents

Charts

Preface and acknowledgments

The origin of this book is partly in a comment made by an anonymous reviewer to a manuscript about the various spiritual disciplines of India, which was submitted to a journal on religion and spirituality. The comment was in response to a sentence I had casually penned in the manuscript saying that the Yogic technique involves a process of retracing the course of one's development. The reviewer had taken me to task for making a bland statement without providing any support. This comment got me thinking. Later on, in the course of correspondence with Professor Thimmappa, a scholar well versed in psychoanalysis and Yoga, the concept of regression popped up. Given his positive response, I started seriously taking the apparent similarities between Freud's view of tracing the course of the development of personality to early childhood on the one hand, and the Yogic concept of the *prati-prasava* on the other. While the Yogic view in this matter seemed quite clear, a chance encounter with some ideas of Sandor Ferenczi, once a close follower and colleague of Freud, prompted me to explore the roots of Freud's view of regression. More recently, my exploration into the literature on the relevance of the Kabbalist mysticism in shaping Freud's worldview provided more food for thought. The present book is the result of such serendipitous stumbling along the line.

I have dedicated this book to the memory of Professor Erik H. Erikson. It was a bit of an accident that I met him during his visit to Pune, India, where he had come in the mid-sixties in search of some references he needed in connection with his book on Gandhi. For some reason I had previously encountered his paper on the problem of ego identity. I was fascinated by his ideas and had written a paper based on my observations from interviews, which I conducted as part of a longitudinal study of youth in which I was working as a research associate. Such coincidences eventually resulted in my working with Prof. Erikson as a post-doctoral fellow under a Fulbright and Smith Mundt grant in 1966–67. For many years my focus in his work remained mostly on his ideas of psycho-social development, and not on psychoanalysis or Freud as such. A few years after my post-doctoral work on identify formation in youth got published, my focus turned increasingly on the concept of identity in Indian thought. In the mid-seventies I went to see Professor Erikson at his residence in Tiburon, just north of San Francisco in California. At that time, I spoke to him about a sharp contrast between the focus on incessant change in the process of human development in his model on the one hand, and the notion in Yoga of an unchanging foundation underlying the continually changing perceptions of the self on the other. Displaying his distinctively open mind, Professor Erikson encouraged me to explore such contrasts. It is his encouragement that led me to work for many subsequent years, leading to a book titled *Self and Identity in Modern Psychology and Indian Thought*. My recent foray into Freud's ideas is a continuation of such comparative cross-cultural studies of concepts in psychology. I need to confess, though, that my understanding of Freud is not based on any experience of psychoanalytic encounters, as I never sought to be a training analyst or even a clinical psychologist.

I met Professor David Bakan after a lecture of his which I had arranged at Simon Fraser University. I was fascinated by his many writings exploring roots of ideas in their historical and cultural background. This was sometime in the late seventies. A long conversation with him led me to an impression of him as a serious scholar, a deep thinker, and a kind human being. I asked him if he would care to read a book manuscript which I had then written. He not only read it but liked and recommended it for publication in the PATH series of books. This resulted in my publication of *Theoretical Psychology: The Meeting of East and West*. This was not the only way in which I benefited from Professor Bakan's kindness; he indeed was one of my mentors. His book on the influence of Judaism on Freud's work has been one of the books that I have found most fascinating; it is the main source of my interest in Jewish mysticism.

There are many old and new friends who have helped me in working on this book by way of encouraging, giving valuable suggestions, cautioning where I could go wrong, correcting me where appropriate, providing references and even entire copies of sharable content, giving critical comments on earlier drafts, and so on and on. I wish to list them (alphabetically!) with an expression of deep gratitude: Brian Ruppenthal, Christiane Hartnack, Doug Oman, Girishwar Misra, Jyotsna Agrawal, Kiran Kumar Salagame, Kundan Singh, Raghu Ananthanarayanan, Rahul Shidhaye, Robert Waxman, Sanford Drob, Sudhir Kakar, and Thimmappa, M.S. In addition, I am also grateful to a couple of anonymous reviewers of an earlier draft of the manuscript, which they not only approved for publication, but also gave constructive criticism which has been helpful. While all of them have helped in bringing out a better piece of work than would have been possible for me to produce single handedly, for all its shortcomings and flaws, I am solely responsible.

Working on this book would not have been possible without the unfailing support in obtaining a variety of reading materials at the Bennett Library at Simon Fraser University, particularly Yolanda Koscielski, who is subject specialist for psychology, and all members of the Inter-Library-Loan department.

There are several personnel at Routledge who have helped in their specialized ways. Among them I wish to specifically mention Lubna Irfan and Brinda Sen.

Anand Paranjpe

Pronunciation and transliteration of Sanskrit terms

Transliteration of Sanskrit terms used in this book follows the commonly used format. For diacritical marks, standard Unicode symbols from Microsoft Word are used. A guide for pronunciation of the sounds represented by the diacritics is given in the following table.

a as in *u* in cut	e as *ay* in say
ā as *a* in far	ai somewhat like *ai* in isle
i as *i* in fit	o as *o* in go
ī as *ee* in see	ou or au as *ou* in out
u as *u* in put	ṁ or ṅ nasalizes the preceding vowel
ṛ somewhat like *r* in bird	ḥ sounds like h with a sharp exhalation of air

The consonants are generally similar to English with a few exceptions. There is a series of "alviolars" (t, th, d, dh, n) pronounced with the tongue touching the gum ridge, and a series of retroflex sounds (ṭ, ṭh, ḍ, ḍh, ṇ) are produced by curling the tongue backwards. The c sounds like *ch* in chair, j as *j* in jug, ś like *sh* in shirt, ñ sounds like ñ in Spanish señor and ṅ like *n* in king.

Introduction

Regression is one of the concepts Freud is known for introducing in modern psychology.[1] It has been redefined and interpreted differently throughout the history of psychoanalysis, particularly in psychoanalytical ego psychology. Interestingly, the concept of *prati-prasava*, which implies a form of regression, also happens to be a critical concept in Yoga psychology. Psychoanalysis and Yoga psychology originated in times eons apart, and in regions continents apart. On the face of it, given the vast differences in time and place that separates them, serious attempts at comparing them would appear to be uncalled for. Yet such attempts have been repeatedly made since Schitz's (1923) book in German back in the early days of psychoanalysis. Girindrasekhar Bose's (1957) book appeared in the 1950s, while Krusche and Desikachar's (2014) book was published less than a decade ago. The search for some commonality in concepts of regression in Indian and Western psychologies is of great interest. A closer look at the apparent similarities can have deep implications for the theory and practice of psychology. As such, this book addresses a closer examination of the concepts of regression and *prati-prasava*.

At the outset I wish to enter a caveat; in juxtaposing the concepts of regression and *prati-prasava* I am by no means claiming their equivalence. Coming from highly diverse contexts, there are some significant differences which will be clarified in the body of this book. The main point connecting the two terms follows mainly from the etymological root of the word regression from Latin *regressus* meaning to go back or return. More specifically, the idea of going back as implied in Freud's technique of exploring the memories of early childhood is crucial, although in Freud's scheme regression acquired a specific (mostly negative) connotation as we shall presently see. In addition to select aspects of the Freudian "classical" psychoanalysis I add to this discussion the ideas of Ernst Kris and Erik Erikson. This is because, while Freud viewed regression as returning to more "primitive" forms of psychic development, both Kris and Erikson deal with the benign

DOI: 10.4324/9781003279860-1

and beneficial aspects of regression. Within the limits of this short book, I limit myself mainly to these authors, and do not extend the discussion to the proliferation of psychoanalytic thought from Jung, Klein, Kohut, Winnicott, Lacan, and a long list of other scholars and practitioners who have immensely enriched the Freudian legacy. As for Yoga I am also restricting myself to mainly Patañjali and wish not to include any developments in Yoga psychology over the past two millennia.

I begin with the psychoanalytical perspective on regression first, as it is likely to be familiar to many readers, and then introduce the Yogic perspective, followed by a discussion comparing the implications of the two concepts.

Note

1 I am grateful to Professor Thimmappa for pointing out the parallel between the concept of regression in Freudian psychanalysis and that of *prati-prasava* in Yoga. This was an added impetus to my long-standing hunch that reversing the evolutionary process is implied in various forms of *sādhanā* in Indian spirituality.

1 The concept of regression in psychoanalysis

The concept of regression in *classical* psychoanalysis

Freud (1920) discussed the concept of regression in the 22nd lecture of his *Introductory lectures on psychoanalysis*. In Freud's model of the structure of the psyche, repression is a key concept, followed by the concepts of regression and fixation, among others. To understand this group of related concepts it is necessary to first recognize that Freud rejected the assumption of the asexual nature of childhood, and emphasized the erotic nature of sucking, biting, defecating, as well as masturbation in children in the first five years of childhood. The basic premise is that parents often discourage, and even threaten to punish stimulation of the phallus or clitoris which children find pleasurable and frequently engage in. It is not uncommon for parents to threaten a little boy to cut off his penis leading to castration anxiety. Another common problem of boys of age around two to five is their wish to be cuddled by the mother and to sleep in her bed. As fathers tend to sleep with the mother and force the son to sleep elsewhere, sons tend to hate their father. The sons' love for their mother and even wishing to marry the mother led Freud to name little boys' love for mother after the Greek myth of Oedipus and conceive of the emotional problems resulting from this situation as the Oedipus complex. All this is well known to not only students of psychology but to the wider public as these Freudian ideas have acquired a wide currency.

The concept of repression arose against this background. Freud recognized that fear of castration and hatred for the father for denying one's place in the mother's attention and bed are strong emotions. It is in understanding the boy's response to such emotions that Freud proposed a "structural model" of the psyche, which recognizes levels of consciousness, namely: wakeful consciousness, associated with the ego, at the top, and preconscious (Pcs) level consciousness at the next level "below" consciousness, and the unconscious (Ucs) at the bottom of the psyche (Freud, 1920, p. 425). For

DOI: 10.4324/9781003279860-2

Freud the entire psyche belonged to the Id, which is composed of impulses derived from instinctual drives, and he conceived of the Ego as an agency of the Id equipped with consciousness and thinking (or secondary processes) (Freud, 1923). It is within this elaborate "structural" model of the psyche that Freud conceived of the boy's response to the strong emotions of fear of castration and hatred for father as a process of repression whereby the unpleasant emotions are "pushed back" from the zone of consciousness into the zone of unconsciousness (Ucs).

Repression is a key concept in the Freudian model. The Id-impulses were implicitly conceived as physical forces and these forces were metaphorically viewed as steam enclosed in a pressure chamber which is waiting to push out when the lid gets loose, allowing it to escape outside the chamber. To extend the physical metaphor of the steam, according to the law of conservation of energy, the forces of repressed drive impulses are supposed to remain stored until they find an escape route. In a related physical metaphor, the steam will find any alternative outlets, like tubes in a container of water. Here the alternative routes could be symbols, as in dreams where a scary person would appear symbolically as a ghost or an animal. Thus, in two famous cases described in detail by Freud, namely the case of Little Hans (Freud, 1909) and Wolf Man (Freud, 1918 [1914]), the fear of the father originating from the Oedipal conflict around the age of five remained repressed, and the fearful father appeared in dreams, in the guise of a horse, in the case of Little Hans. The persistent irrational fear or phobia of horses or wolves was explained by Freud as obsessive-compulsive neurosis. According to Freud such neuroses continue well into adulthood as the pent-up emotions continue to be trapped in the underground chamber of the unconscious region of the Id. Psychoanalytic therapy was based on this model. It was thought that once the patient was given to understand that his fear was not of an animal, but that of the father, then this insight was thought to be adequate in bringing the repressed fear out from the unconscious to the conscious domain of the Ego. The "pressure" was thus released and the phobic reaction against an animal disappeared.[1]

Freud's concept of regression is in the context of his model of the psyche as explained previously. In Freud's view, while the patient often develops neurotic symptoms as a result of the repression of childhood fears or hatred, the Ego may adopt two different strategies. *First*, the person may get *fixated* – that is, stuck, so to speak – at the same stage at which the neurotic symptom originated; at the Oedipal stage around age five, for instance (Little Hans was lucky to be relived from his phobia very early since his father consulted Freud when Hans was still a little boy). *Second*, alternatively, a patient may go back to an earlier stage of development, or *regress*. In the case of Wolf Man, for example, the patient *regressed*, meaning that he went back to an earlier stage of his psycho-sexual development – that of anal expulsive stage where a child of about two or three years of age derives pleasure from the process of excretion. Thus, Wolf Man's regression resulted in his being cruel to animals; it is as if the hatred for parents arising at the stage of toilet training was projected onto helpless animals as a substitute object.

It should be clear now as to how fixation as well as regression are viewed in a negative light, since both forms of response to childhood frustrations are said to commonly result in obsessive compulsive or other forms of neuroses.

At this point it would be useful to note that the strategy of regression as a form of "turning back" has two related forms: *first*, in the form of Freud's strategy to look for clues for causes underlying neurotic symptoms buried in the past history of the patient, and *second*, regression as a form of reverting to an adaptive mode typical of an earlier stage of psycho-sexual development. Nevertheless, the focus is on the early years of life after birth. It may be noted, however, that Freud's gaze into the past is not limited to the life of the individual since birth. There are several instances where Freud mentions the origin of symptoms of regression to events prior to the birth of the individual. Thus, in Chapter XXII of his *Introductory Lectures on Psychoanalysis* Freud (1920) gives two examples of regression where there were reversals to events prior to the birth of the individuals. In the first example Freud draws an analogy with a history of civilization, where an ancestral community migrates from its domicile to a new one, except some members of the community are left behind at the original location (pp. 421–422). In a second example he suggests that the patient's regression was like going back to the stage of the evolution of fish during the course of phylogenesis. In the context of this example, he tells us about his research under the direction of his research guide Ernst Brücke. That research project indicated how the location of the nerve centers had changed during the course of evolution to different locations in the body (p. 422). Thus, the shifting of a patient's position from a later stage of development to an earlier stage is like the sifting of location of bodily parts of an organism during the course of evolution. Elsewhere in Freud's writings we find a reference to the then-prevailing idea that the changes during the span of life of an organism (ontogenesis) involve a pattern similar to the changes in the course of the evolution of the species (phylogenesis). Given the prevalence of this idea in the community of scientists in Freud's environment, it would hardly be surprising if Freud could stretch the timeline for regression to the evolutionary history of the human species.

To put it simply, the timeline for Freud's concept or regression goes well beyond the birth of the individual – although one often gets the impression that he thought of going back in the history of the individual only to early childhood since his famous case studies are based primarily on childhood memories. The reason to emphasize the issue of the extension of the time-line is that, as we shall see toward the end of this book, the roots of the idea may possibly be found on the influence on Freud of the Jewish Kabbalah, where the time line stretches back to Genesis and the origin of humanity, when God created the world. Indeed, there is reference in Freud's writings which gives rise to a suspicion that he may have possibly derived his view of regression from his background in Jewish mysticism. Thus, in his book *Beyond the pleasure principle* he says:

> But for the moment it is tempting to pursue to its logical conclusion the hypothesis that all instincts tend towards the restoration of an earlier state of things. The outcome may give an impression of mysticism or of sham profundity; but we can feel quite innocent of having had any such purpose in view.
>
> (Freud, 1922, p. 37)

Note how Freud makes a sweeping statement saying that *all* instincts tend toward the *restoration to an earlier state of things*. Then he suspects that readers may think that he is deriving this hypothesis from some form of *mysticism*, and quickly declares that there is no such connection. This fits in with Freud's consistent and careful repudiation of any sort of mysticism or religion for that matter. We shall return to the issue of Freud's alleged connection with the Kabbalist mysticism to which he was exposed since his childhood.

Another issue regarding Freud's view of regression which deserves attention is that his immediate followers, including his daughter Anna, presented a different perspective on the idea of regression. The work of Ernst Kris (1950, 1952) is particularly relevant in this context since he pointed out some of the *beneficial* aspects of regression in contrast to such *negative* aspects of regression as getting fixated at an earlier and less desirable level during the course of the development of personality. As is well known, Freud's followers modified the "classical" model as presented in his work in many different directions. Here we may turn to one of the many revisions of the classical model in the work of Anna Freud and her close associates, leading to what has been called "psychoanalytical ego psychology".

The concept of regression in *psychoanalytical ego psychology*

As noted, Freud's view of regression was inextricably connected with his view of the Ego and the Id. In the Freudian model, Ego is basically a servant of its master, the Id. The purpose of the Ego is essentially to allow the amoral demands of instinctual impulses by fending off the moralist dictates of the Super Ego one the one side, and the demands of the real world on the outside. The Ego in the Freudian model is thus perpetually involved in a conflict with the Id and the Superego. As David Rapaport (1959) points out in his introduction to Erikson's (1959) monograph titled *Identity and the Life Cycle*, Freud's view of the Ego as perpetually involved in a conflict was not acceptable to Freud's daughter Anna and a group of her colleagues. They conceived of a "conflict-free sphere of the ego" and founded a new school of psychoanalysis called ego psychoanalytical psychology. Ernst Kris and Erik Erikson were members of this group along with Heinz Hartmann and Rudolph Loewenstein among others. The work of Ernst Kris deserves special attention in view of the changing perspectives on the role of regression in the development of personality.

Ernst Kris (1952) introduced the important concept of the "regression in service of the ego". Kris's main interest was on creativity in art, particularly in painting and other forms of the visual arts such as drawing caricatures. His entire book was concerned about the role of the preconscious in dreams, humor, caricatures, and painting. In his view, regression to early childhood experiences opens up a door for creativity in the zone of the preconscious in a way that consciousness does not allow. Assisting in the creative process in the production of art is thus a *positive outcome* of regression as distinguished from the negative role of reverting to the unconscious and preconscious zones of the psyche which Freud had emphasized. That is how, in Kris's opinion, regression *serves* the ego. Moreover, Kris thought that artists can use the strengths of the ego to *deliberately* regress into the preconscious so as to release their creative potential in producing works of art. Thus, in Kris's perspective on psychoanalysis, Freud's idea of the Ego as a servant of the Id is radically reversed. Unlike the Ego in Freud's view as a servant of the Id, the ego as conceived in Kris's scheme can not only benefit from regression – it can also be strong enough to *initiate* a process of regression and reap its benefits. Kris sums up his view of regression and ego in the last sentence of his book *Psychoanalytic Explorations in Art* as follows:

> The relationship between creativity and passivity exemplifies once more of the leading thesis of this presentation: the integrative functions of the ego include *self-regulated regression* and permit a combination of the most daring intellectual activity with the experience of passive receptiveness.
>
> (Kris, 1952, p. 318; emphasis added)

It is useful to note Kris's reference to the "most daring intellectual activity" of the Ego. In this instance, Kris's view of the psyche indicates a significant departure from Freud's view of the dominance of irrationality in the working of the psyche.

Erik Erikson, who did his training in psychoanalysis under the guidance of Anna Freud, advanced the work of Anna and Kris, while following in particular the work of Hartmann, Kris, and Loewenstein (1946) in two significant ways: First, he emphasized the autonomy and agency of the Ego, and second, he recognized the influence of society on the individual, and extended the psycho-*sexual* development of the child up to adolescence to eight stages of psycho-*social* development through the entire life cycle. Here we need not be concerned about Erikson's extensive work on the development of the person from the cradle to the grave; we need to focus only on his views of regression and on *ego-identity*, which is the central concept of his work. As to the concept of regression, there are several references to it in the context of his clinical work with occasional references to Kris's views about regression in service of the Ego. As I hunted through the list of references to the term regression in his many books, I got the impression that he seemed to be comfortable in recognizing the beneficial usage of regression in the form of investigating events of earlier childhood. In this regard he followed Freud's lead. However, his discomfort in its use becomes manifest in his comments on the analysis of dreams. Thus, he says in his book *Insight and Responsibility*: "The dreamer's ego, consequently, appears in no way 'regressed' – a term often thoughtlessly used when speaking of a dream's return to infantile wishes and frustration" (Erikson, 1964, p. 184). Immediately after writing these words, he continues with a longer sentence in which he speaks of the autonomy of the Ego and some positive gains in looking back at earlier stages in life in the following way:

> Rather, the dreamer returns to his earliest dealings with (and subsequent reiterations of) one of life's major themes, and he thinks himself forward again, through a number of stages, convincing himself that each mournful loss and each frightening graduation brings with it an increased autonomy and an enhanced ability to find in adult actuality the resources of competence and tradition.
>
> (p. 184)

Here, as we can see, ego psychoanalysis has come far away from its Freudian roots. It is not only the autonomy of the ego that is clearly mentioned – the Ego also is viewed as able to use resources of the individual's competence, as well the resources of the *tradition* to which the person belongs. Moreover, here Erikson is speaking not simply about a dreamer but also about a person wide awake, who is mulling over "major themes" in her/his life. The Freudian focus on the weakness and eternally conflicted nature of the Ego is left behind. As is well known, Erikson develops the concept of ego and focuses on the *identity* – meaning the continued *sameness* – of the “I” and examines in detail the process of *identity formation.*

Before examining Erikson’s view of identity formation, it is necessary to clarify two related, but distinct, meanings of the critical term “identity” to help understand what exactly Erikson means by its use. *First*, in Erikson’s work as in common language, the term identity connotes a person’s feelings of *identification* with something or other, particularly identification with one’s thoughts, self-images, social roles within groups/communities to which one belongs, as also with ingroup’s values, shared ideals, and ideology. This is the sense in which we use the expression Freud’s Jewish identity, or Erikson’s American identity as an immigrant in America, and so on. It is in this context that Erikson speaks of the *psycho-social* identity of a person. The *second* meaning of the term identity is *the condition of being the same*. Thus, in geometry we can say that the two triangles are identical; they have all the *same* properties lacking any distinction. There is a sense in which a person can say that I am the *same* person as I was as a toddler, although both myself and my older acquaintances recognize that there is much difference also between me as a toddler then and as an adult now. Such usage of the term is called *identity-in-difference*, and this is implied in the notion of *personal identity*.

To say that something is the *same*, and also that it has *changed*, implies acceptance of two opposites to be true *at the same time*, which is a paradox. This paradox is known as an enigma of “personal identity”. In the history of Western thought several philosophers including in particular John Locke (1690/1959) and Immanuel Kant (1781/1966) have tried to solve the paradox of identity. William James (1890/1983) examined and critiqued their views. (For a detailed discussion of the concept identity and its implications see Paranjpe, 1998.) Indeed, James came close to accepting Kant’s notion of the transcending aspect of ego, which he justified mainly on rational grounds. But Erikson, as a practicing clinical psychologist, was interested more in how persons *cope* with continual and ceaseless change in their lives across decades than in trying to find out *what*, if anything, remains the same in a person from cradle to grave. Moreover, as a developmental psychologist, he presented a perspective on the nature of change through the life cycle, and the way in which individuals develop a *sense* of being the same person in the following words:

> From a genetic [i.e., developmental] point of view, then, the process of identity formation emerges as an *evolving configuration* – a configuration which is gradually established by successive ego-syntheses and resyntheses throughout childhood; it is a configuration gradually

> integrating *constitutional givens, idiosyncratic libidinal needs, favored capacities, significant identifications, effective defenses, successful sublimations, and consistent roles.*
>
> (Erikson, 1959, p. 116; italics original)

Beyond offering such a descriptive analysis of the nature of ongoing change in people's lives, Erikson tried to explain how most people develop a "sense" of self-sameness or a sense of "identity" while continuing to cope with ongoing change. Here is how he puts it:

> An increasing sense of identity is preconsciously experienced as a "sense of psychosocial well-being". . . . Such a sense of identity, however, is never gained nor maintained once and for all. Like a "good conscience" it is constantly lost and regained, although more lasting and more economical methods of maintenance and restoration are evolved and fortified in late adolescence.
>
> (Erikson, 1959, p. 118)

This conclusion indicates that, according to Erikson, most people seem to attain only a "sense" of being the same person without actually finding anything that guarantees continued sameness. It is something that is only "preconsciously experienced", and not a clear and conscious experience – let alone a conviction founded on an indubitable experience. Nevertheless, in one of his later works titled *Identity Youth and Crisis*, Erikson (1968) hints at something that could explain as to wherein lies a foundation of selfsameness. Thus, he says "there is more to a man's core than identity, that there is in fact in each individual an 'I,' an observing center of awareness and of volition, which can transcend and must survive the *psychosocial identity*, which is the concern of this book" (p. 135; italics original.) Nevertheless, it is important to note that Erikson recognized a sense of identity as a preconscious experience, implicitly admitting that a person who arrives at such a sense does so without actually finding or discovering *what* it is it in a person that remains the same.[2]

Erikson does not say anything more about the "transcendental center of awareness" – if and how such a principle could be discovered, and if it is then what good it may do to a person who discovers it. The reason to note the lack of elaboration about the nature of such a principle is simply that, according to Patañjali, one can discover an unshakable foundation of self-sameness through the successful practice of Yoga. Moreover, the experience of an unchanging Self underlying continuing changes in the images of the self are said to end a continuing chase of ever new images of the self, leading to an everlasting inner peace and bliss. Interestingly, Patañjali

(2006) (2.10)[3] also suggests *prati-prasava*, a certain form of regression, as a way to discover the transcendental Self though the experience of higher states of consciousness.

Notes

1 For a detailed analysis of Freud's case study of Little Hans and insight into the nature of symbolism as the means for cure, see Roger Brown (1965).

2 In this context, I would like to mention that in a personal conversation with Professor Erikson at his residence in Tiburon, California, in about 1975, he effectively admitted that the issue of sameness remains elusive. I told him in that conversation that Patañjali speaks about discovering an unchanging true Self through meditation. When I asked him if it was worth pursuing the basis for such major differences in perspectives on the issue of what remains the same in continually changing perceptions of selfhood, he said yes.

3 There are numerous English translations of Patañjali's *Yoga Sūtras* available. For a translation of the original text, along with commentaries of Vyāsa and Vācaspati Miśra, I have primarily used a very recent translation by Gerald Larson (2018), and for translation of original aphorisms and commentaries by Vyāsa and Vijñānabhikṣu I have relied on T.S. Rukmani (1980-1989). I have also found Taimni's (2007) book useful. As to the Sanskrit texts I have relied mainly on K.S. Arjunwadkar (2006).

2 Conceptual foundations of Yoga

Basic concepts of Sāṁkhya and Yoga

The Sāṁkhya system postulates two distinct ontological categories: the sentient Puruṣa as distinguished from insentient Prakṛti, which is basically a principle of materiality underlying the visible/tangible reality. While the Puruṣa is an unchanging, uninvolved, and non-agentic witness of what goes on in the domain of the observable world, there is incessant change in the domain of Prakṛti. The changes in the observable world are said to be the result of the continual mutual interaction among three of its constituents or "strands" (*guṇa*s) of Prakṛti. There are no exact equivalents of these "strands" in Western thought, but some closely equivalent concepts may be cited. (For a discussion of the concept of the three *guṇa*s of Sāṁkhya and some parallels in Western thought, see Paranjpe, 1983.) Thus, *sattva* is the "intelligent" stuff, *rajas* is "energy", and *tamas* is more like "inertia" or "mass".

Puruṣa is basically conceived as one single principle along with its twin, the Prakṛti. However, Īśvarakṛṣṇa, the author of the *Sāṁkhya Kārikā*, unambiguously states (in *kārikā*, or stanza, 18)[1] that there are many *puruṣa*s. As the same word *Puruṣa* is used in Sanskrit as written in the Devanāgarī script as पुरुष to designate both the single *Puruṣa* as well as many *puruṣas*, this equivocation is often confusing. It appears that for those who read the texts in Sanskrit this may not be much of a problem as they may be able to easily figure out the correct meaning in context. Nevertheless, the two meanings of the same term, one implying singularity and the other multiplicity surely needs clarification. I found such a clarification in Hiriyanna's (1948/1995) textbook of Indian philosophy (pp. 108 & 115–16). He points out that the origin of the Sāṁkhyan usage of the Puruṣa as both single and multiple can be traced back to two hymns of the ṚgVeda.

First, the origin of the term Puruṣa can be easily traced to a hymn of the ṚgVeda (10.90) called the *Puruṣa Sūkta*, where Puruṣa is described as a

DOI: 10.4324/9781003279860-3

cosmic Person with a thousand heads, thousand eyes, and feet. More specifically, this Person is said to be an immanent principle of the universe spreading all over, while also transcending it. From this latter description, Puruṣa is the same ubiquitous principle otherwise called Brahman in the Upaniṣads, and as a sentient principle it stands in contrast with the insentient Prakṛti in the Sāṁkhya system. Another hymn of the ṚgVeda (10.129) called the Nāsadīya Sūkta speculates that at the beginning of the universe there was a single principle (*ekam*) in which emerged a desire (*kāma*) – presumably to create the world. The Upaniṣads follow this ṚgVedic lead in conceptualizing the creation from "One" to "Many". Thus, the Bṛhadāraṇyaka Upaniṣad (1.4.1), which is said to be one of the earliest philosophical texts in the tradition of the Vedas, says: "In the beginning this (world) was only the self, in the shape of a person [*puruṣavidhaḥ*]. Looking around he saw nothing else than the self. He first said 'I am'. Therefore arose the name I" (Radhakrishnan, 1953/1994, p. 163). Following this theme, the Bṛhadāraṇyaka Upaniṣad (1.4.4) continues:

> He, verily, had no delight. Therefore he who is alone has no delight . . . He caused that self to fall into two parts. From that arose husband and wife. . . . From that human beings were produced.
>
> (Radhakrishnan, 1953/1994, p. 164)

The Chāndogya Upaniṣad follows up on this theme of creation. It says: "in the beginning this was being alone, one only, without a second. . . . It thought, May I be many" (Chāndogya Upaniṣad, 6.2.2–3; Radhakrishnan, 1953/1994, p. 449). The Taittirīya Upaniṣad (2.6.1) repeats the phrase used by the Chāndogya: "Let me become many" (*bahu syāṁ prajāyeyeti*; Radhakrishnan, 1953/1994, p. 547).

This background of the ṚgVeda and the Upaniṣads makes it clear that the term Puruṣa has been equated with the concepts of Brahman, the single immanent and transcendent principle of reality. The concept of Puruṣa is also equated with the concept of the Self (*Ātman*). Moreover, the idea of the "One" Self which divided itself into "Many" selves would have been a common part of the intellectual heritage for Īśvarakṛṣṇa in expounding the Sāṁkhya system. We may safely assume that these themes were part of a widely shared tacit knowledge within the Vedic fold without any need for explanation or even a mention. The same situation with tacit understanding would continue when Patañjali followed the Sāṁkhya system. Since it is taken for granted that it was the same "One" that begat the "Many", then they would take on the same family name – as was common in patriarchal societies. For those familiar with the Upaniṣadic lore, it may be instantly clear whether, in a given context, the term Puruṣa refers to the single principle of the One Self (Puruṣa) or a particular individual self among many selves (*puruṣa*s).

So much, then, for the equivocation in the two meanings of the term Puruṣa. To help contemporary readers, I am using, following William James (1890/1993), the notation Puruṣa with a Capital P to designate Puruṣa as the single pervasive and all-encompassing and transcendental principle, and a twin of Prakṛti, and use *puruṣa* with a lower-case p to designate the countless living beings or "embodied souls" (*śārīra ātmā* or *bhūtātmā* in the Upaiṣadic phraseology).

The Sāṁkhyan view of the evolution of the "Many" from the "One"

Aside from these basic concepts, the Sāṁkhya offers a specific perspective on the evolution of the universe within the domain of Prakṛti. Since the notion of *prati-prasava* as a form of *regression* or involution going in a direction opposite to evolution is conceived by Sāṁkhya, it is necessary to understand the Sāṁkhyan view of evolution. It is but natural that the same landmarks appear in a journey whether one proceeds forward or backward. The concepts used to describe those landmarks are therefore crucial in understanding the yogi's journey on the path to *Kaivalya* as regression. The basic idea of cosmic evolution according to Sāṁkhya is schematically represented in Chart 2.1.

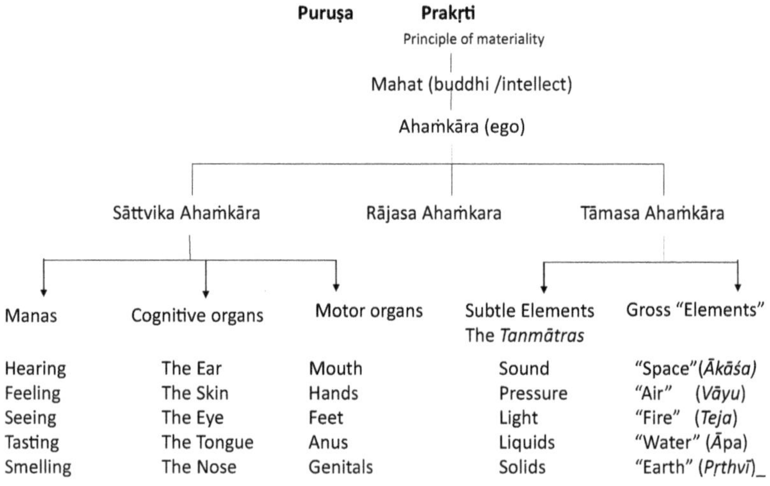

Chart 2.1 Schematic view of cosmic evolution according to Sāṁkhya

As indicated in Chart 2.1, the first product of Prakṛti in the course of its evolution is called Mahat or the Great One. This is the stage of individuation, or formation of separate individual living beings. Each of these individual beings is thought to be equipped with some form of "intelligence" (*buddhi*), which helps them to maneuver their way through the surrounding world. It makes sense, then, as to why Mahat is also called *buddhi*. The immediate next step is the emergence of ego, implying the separation of the self from the world or the other. After this stage, the course of evolution is said to take two rather separate courses of development. While one is guided by one of the three "strands" of Prakṛti called *sattva*, which involves an illuminating function, the second one is guided by the strand called *tamas* or inertia. The mind is said to emerge from *sattva*, and the body from *tamas*. According to Dasgupta (1922/1975, Vol. I, p. 241) *sattva* has a special quality of translucence which resembles the illuminating quality of the Puruṣa and thereby absorbs and reflects the consciousness of Puruṣa – albeit in a compromised rather than full form. The third "strand" called *rajas* straddles across the two paths guided by *sattva*/mind on the one side and the *tamas*/body on the other, energizing both mind and body. From here on the course of evolution turns to the rise of subtle elements called the *tattva*s. The concept of *tattva* is difficult to explain and interpret, although several good sources are helpful (Dasgupta, 1924/1973; Larson & Bhattacharya, 1987/2006; Parrott, 1986; Dobson, 1979/1983). It is not necessary to go into the details of the concept of *tattva*, but a short explanation regarding their role in the process of regression (*prati-prasava*) is in order.

As pointed out by Parrott (1986), the Sāṁkhya *tattva*s are both cosmic and psychological phenomena. Their conceptualization involves a totally psycho-physical conception of reality; it is unlike the Cartesian dualism which conceives of mind and matter as radically unlike entities. As psycho-physical entities, the *tattva*s are similar to Leibniz's *monad*s, which are both unextended like thoughts, as well as extended like material particles, at the same time. The *tattva*s are said to evolve as Prakṛti unfolds, giving rise to the psychological functions on the "subtle" side and as physical "elements" on the "gross" side. As Larson and Bhattacharya (1987/2006) put it: "The subtle elements are generic presuppositions for the experience of specific objectivity". For example, they point out that "The subtle sound element itself is not any particular sound, it is the generic essence of sound . . . the universal possibility of sound-as-such" (p. 58). Although there are attempts to interpret the *tattva*s in terms of contemporary physics (Dobson, 1979/1983; Duquette, 2010), such interpretations are problematic since the Cartesian and Sāṁkhyan worldviews are largely non-commensurable.

Some of the problems in understanding the nature of the Sāṁkhya *tattva*s become obvious if we just take a look at the standard list of the five "gross elements" and their common translations in English: *ākāśa* (space, ether), *vāyu* (wind, air), *teja* (fire), *āp* (water), *pṛthvī* (earth). The common translation of *pṛthvī* as earth is misleading since in current times earth is commonly understood as the planet visible from the moon and outer space. The translation is wrong because it does not convey the sense in which it means an "element" in the Sāṁkhya system. This is certainly not what the Sāṁkhya system means by the term *pṛthvī*. The meaning of *pṛthvī* is more like matter or mass. Then there is the problem of how the gross elements of Sāṁkhya are thought of as elements in comparison to those listed in Mendeleev's Periodic Table of chemical elements as understood in modern chemistry. A comparison between Sāṁkhyan "gross elements" and elements of modern chemistry is misleading and unnecessary. What is important to understand is that, as Parrott (1986, p. 58) points out, the Sāṁkhya philosophers observed the physical world by reaching out to it through the powers of the senses, and conceived of *tattva*s as psycho-physical entities – not as purely physical entities like the elements of modern chemistry. Conceived in strictly psychophysical terms, the *tattva*s find a specific place in the Yoga system in the light of the experiential universe which is said to open up to an advanced yogi through successful practice of the techniques of Yoga. According to Yogic texts, the *tattva*s are accessible to observation by advanced yogis, but inaccessible to persons lacking in the advanced practices of Yoga. To help in understanding the significance of the *tattva*s in the context of the Yogic view of regression (*prati-prasava*), it is necessary to note some more details of the concept of the *tattva*s, and the way they are placed in a hierarchical structure.

The hierarchical structure of the *tattva*s relates to their sequential origination in time order, which is represented in series of *columns* from top to bottom as indicated in Chart 2.1. The texts use the word "*kramaśaḥ*" meaning the successive (or diachronic) order of their evolution. This is to be distinguished from a synchronic development (*yugapad*) represented in *rows* in Chart 2.1. It makes sense to view synchronic or side-by-side development, for instance, in the case of sound such that the experiential capacity for *sensing* auditory signals must develop side-by-side with the development of matching capacity of the *auditory organ* in the body, or else the organisms would not be able to use their auditory capacities to adapt to their environment. In Chart 2.1 the synchronic and side-by-side development of the sensory/cognitive capacities and matching capacities of sensory and motor organs is indicated by placing them in horizontal rows. (I am not sure, however, about the parallel development of the *motor* organs.) At any rate, there is an aspect of the diachronic emergence of the *tattva*s that is particularly important in understanding *prati-prasava*, since this Yogic form of regression involves going in the direction opposite to the evolution of the *tattva*s.

In one of the few alternative versions of the Sāṁkhya system there is an "accumulation theory" of the successive development of the five *tattva*s according to which each successive *tattva* combines with the preceding ones in order to generate a grosser element (Larson & Bhattacharya, 1987/2006, p. 51). Thus, the first *tattva* to emerge in the course of evolution is *śabda tanmātra* (of sound) coming from *ākāśa* or "space". Then the sequence goes as indicated in Chart 2.2:

1. *Śabda -> (auditory)*
2. *Śabda + sparśa -> (tactile)*
3. *Śabda + sparśa + rūpa -> (visual)*
4. *Śabda + sparśa + rūpa + rasa -> (gustatory)*
5. *Śabda + sparśa + rūpa + rasa + gandha -> (olfactory)*

Chart 2.2 The cumulative development of *tattva*s

This accumulative development implies that each subsequent *tattva* is *added* to the previous ones in such a way that the next is more comprehensive and increasingly gross. In other words, the course of evolution goes from relatively abstract to increasingly concrete and comprehensive *tattva*s. The reason for going into this detail is that, as we will see later, the yogi is said to advance in her/his spiritual development in a direction *opposite* to their formation as indicated earlier. We may leave the Sāṁkhyan background at this point and proceed with an account of Patañjali's Yoga.

The eight "limbs" (*aṣṭāṅga*) of Patañjali's Yoga

As is widely known, Patañjali proposes the following "limbs" of Yoga.

(1) *Yama*: a set of behavioral *restraints* such as non-violence, avoidance of telling lies etc.,
(2) *Niyama*: a set of *observances*, such as cleanliness, cultivation of a sense of contentment, ascetic practices, Self-study, and surrendering fruits of action to God,
(3) *Āsana*: a steady and comfortable *posture*,
(4) *Prāṇāyāma*: *breath control*,
(5) *Pratyāhāra: withdrawing of attention* from objects of the senses,
(6) *Dhārṇā*: *restricting the range of attention* or concentration,
(7) *Dhyāna*: *sustaining attention* for a length of time, or contemplation,
(8) *Samādhi*: a graded series of increasingly *higher states of consciousness*.

The reason to use the term "limb" as translation of "*aṅga*" is that the eight items listed are neither simply aspects, nor steps to be taken strictly in that sequence across time. They are, rather, integral to Yoga in a manner in which limbs of a body work together and jointly constitute the whole. It is not correct to assume that all the eight "limbs" must be practiced in a strict succession in which they are listed in the *Yoga Sūtra* 2.29 (and as listed previously). As pointed out by R.S. Bhattacharya (1976), the first two limbs, the *Yama*s and *Niyama*s, are ethical principles that respectively proscribe unethical behaviors and prescribe good ones, and these principles must be practiced *all the time* by a practitioner of Yoga. They are therefore to be practiced concurrently, not in sequence. The postures and modes of breath control *can* be practiced without moral preparation as indeed many people *do*, although there is no prescription as such. As Yoga has spread across the world, aspects of Yoga – mainly postures or *āsanas*, and a bit of breath control or *prāṇāyāma* – have been commodified and are "sold" in studios for a fee. There are, indeed, several benefits which follow from their practice, and the benefits are being measured in numerous often reasonably sophisticated research projects, and their results are being reviewed (e.g., de Michelis, 2007; Cramer, Lauche, & Dobos, 2014). But in the middle of all this, while *āsana* and *prāṇāyāma* are focused upon, the ethical guidelines comprising of the first two "limbs" are conveniently ignored.

As to the common disdain for the ethical guidelines of the *Yamas* and the *Niyamas*, Kenneth Liberman (2008) has made an apt observation: "The situation today is that less than a small percentage of yoga students in the world can correctly identify the yamas and niyamas, let alone practice them. This is a scandal" (p. 112). On the other side of *āsana* and *prāṇāyāma* in the standard list of the eight "limbs" of Patañjali's *Aṣṭāṅga Yoga*, is the fifth "limb" called the *pratyāhāra*, in which a yogic practitioner is required to withdraw her attention from the "outside" world of objects and turn it into the inner world of the mind's contents and processes. With that maneuver starts the difficult march of the *Dhyāna Yoga* to its goal, *Kaivalya*. This inner core (*antaraṅga*) of Yoga has little place in what is often called the "modern Yoga" that is continuing to spread around the globe. It is in this "inner" core of Yoga (which Shri Raghu Ananthanarayanan aptly calls the "Antaranga Yoga")[2] that a Yogi *reverses* the evolutionary trajectory and begins her march "backward" toward the primordial Puruṣa, the "One" with which the entire course of evolution is believed to have started.

Notes

1 *janmamaraṇakaraṇānām pratiniyamād ayugapatpravṛtteśca* | *puruṣabahutvaṁ siddhaṁ traiguṇyaviparyayāccaiva* || (*Sāṁkhya Kārikā*, 18)
2 Ananthanarayanan's book on this topic is forthcoming. Its details were not available until the completion of writing this manuscript.

3 The concept of *prati-prasava*

A Yogic view of regression

Prati-prasava: A yogi's "regression" to the origin of evolution

I am using the word *regression* as applied to the Yogic system as a translation of the term *prati-prasava* mentioned in Patañjali (2.10), which literally means, according to the Monier Williams Dictionary, going in a *counter order*. It should be easy to see that this meaning is pretty much the same as the etymological root of the word regression from Latin *regressus*, meaning to go back or return. In Yoga, it specifically means going back to the primordial or pristine state of the Puruṣa by going counter to the way in which we as countless living beings – *puruṣa*s – are said to have evolved from the "One" Puruṣa. In other words, the idea is that the person (*puruṣa*), who is normally in the wakeful state while starting on the path of Yoga, should go *back* to the nascent state of the Puruṣa which is pure consciousness. The overall thrust of Yoga, as I view it, involves a process or "regression" where the process of meditation takes a meditator in a direction opposite to the direction in which Prakṛti is thought to have evolved into an objective reality accessible to observation through the processes of sensation and cognition. Upon successful completion of meditation, the meditator reaches even beyond the level of Prakṛti to restore the Self as the primordial Person (Puruṣa) in the experience of "pure" or contentless consciousness.

The *Yoga Sūtras* present two or three different, if related, ways in which a meditator "regresses" so as to reach the nascent state of the Self as Seer (*draṣṭā*). The first of these differing ways is encountered in Patañjali's aphorism 1.45 which describes the transition from the first to the second level of Samādhi. The second way for attaining the same goal can be found in the description of how "regression" (*prati-prasava*) can help in going backward through the chain of "afflictions" (*avidyā, asmitā, rāga, dveṣa, abhiniveśa*). These two versions of *prati-prasva* are described one after another in two subsequent sections to follow, once we take another look at the *progression* of the yogic aspirant through the eight "limbs".

DOI: 10.4324/9781003279860-4

An aspirant's progression through the eight "limbs" of Patañjali's "eight-fold" (Aṣṭāṅga) Yoga

The serious practice of avoiding doing harm (*ahimsā*) and stealing (*asteya*), as well as observing other such strictures on behavior suggested in the first "limb" called the Yamas, spares the individual from distractions such as fear of possible retaliation or punishment and so on. This is just a minimum level of preparation in the pursuit of spiritual engagement. The observance of cleanliness and the cultivation of contentedness, which are the first two observances prescribed in the second "limb" called the Niyama, affords a further step in preparation. (The other five items in the list of Niyamas have a special function, which will be described in a later section of this discussion.) The practice of appropriate postures and breath control described in the third and fourth "limbs" prepares stability and the bodily comfort necessary for calming down and concentrating the mind. All this is covered under the "external" or physical aspects of preparation toward the more serious core practices which begin with the withdrawal of attention (*pratyāhāra*) described in the fifth "limb". The withdrawal of attention from the outside world and turning it inward involves a process of *introspection* which is somewhat similar to the strategy prescribed by Wilhelm Wundt, the founder of modern psychology, for looking into the mind. The method of introspection was developed and used from the founding of Wundt's laboratory around 1876 through 1913 when Watson declared it null and void. Beyond the apparent similarity between introspection as prescribed by Wundt and practiced by his followers in Germany and the US, there are major differences between these two strategies, and these differences must be clarified. Such clarification is necessary since, given the bad reputation surrounding the idea of introspection since J.B. Watson (1913), readers familiar with the history of modern psychology could dismiss Yoga as an enterprise founded on a "failed" methodology.

As is well known, Titchener, Wundt's American follower, did not agree about the major findings of introspectionist studies by his German followers like Ach, Marbe, and others (for a review of classical introspection in modern psychology see Boring, 1953, and Bakan, 1954). It is also widely known that the serious disagreements among Wundt's followers led Watson (1913) to declare that the method of introspection was null and void, and launch the behaviorist revolution in modern psychology. Without going into details, it is necessary to point out that the modern "introspectionists" were trying to *observe* and *analyze* the *contents* of consciousness. The idea that the contents of consciousness are composed of elemental units is traced back to John Locke (1690/1959) who suggested that simple ideas originating from sensation combine into complex ideas which make up what and how we know the world. He based this suggestion following his friend Robert Boyle, a pioneer in chemistry, who had initiated the distinction between elements and compounds. Later John Stuart Mill conceived of "mental chemistry" and the laws of combination of simple ideas into complex ideas. The introspectionists' search was guided by these ideas in the background. The problem, however, was with this particular form of the method of introspection, which was different from the nature and use of introspection in Yoga. This is an issue which deserves some discussion.

Well before Wundt launched his program of introspection in modern psychology, the French philosopher August Comte, the founder of the philosophy of positivism, had pointed out a basic problem with the method of internal observation. This was in his *Cours de Philosophie Positive* published between 1830 and 1842, decades before both Wundt and William James founded modern psychology in the 1870s. In fact, in his *Principles of Psychology* William James (1890/1983) quotes Comte while translating the latter's words as follows: "The thinker cannot divide himself in two, of whom one reasons whilst the other observes him reason. The organ observed and the organ observing being, in this case, identical, how could observation take place?" (James, 1890/1983, p. 188). This same difficulty was recognized in ancient times in the Bṛhadāraṇyaka Upaniṣad (4.5.15) where the sage Janaka rhetorically asks the question: "Indeed, by what would one know the knower?" (see Radhakrishnan, 1953/1994, p. 286). Patañjali (4.20) explicitly notes that it is impossible to simultaneously comprehend both the seer and the seen.[1] It is true that, although it is impossible to grasp the thinker and the thought at the same time, it is possible for a current thought to recall the previous thought. In other words, it should be possible to substitute introspection with retrospection. However, since each thought is immediately replaced by another thought, retrospection leads to an infinite regress where one thought chases the next and so on and so on ad infinitum. This difficulty, too, was explicitly recognized by Patañjali (4.21).[2] These references indicate that the ancient forebears of Patañjali must have tried introspection as well as retrospection, recognized the inherent difficulties therein, and had chosen not to adopt a strategy of examining and analyzing the contents of passing thoughts as did the modern introspectionists. Interestingly, the Sāṁkhya-Yoga thinkers *did* conceive elemental units which they called the *tanmātra*s, but these were thought to be psycho-physical entities accessible to advanced yogis, not elements of consciousness observable by ordinary subjects as in the case of Wundt and his followers.

Come to think of it, the idea of retrospection where a current thought examines the contents of a previous thought in the stream of consciousness *can* be viewed as a form of regression. This form of introspection involves looking back across the shortest span of time scale in the ongoing flow of time – a micro-regression, so to speak. On the time scale of Freud's method, looking back at early childhood covers not only just a small portion of a person's life span, but a tiny fraction of the long span of history since the beginning of the universe whatever number of billion years ago. As we shall see, the Yogic as well as Kabbalist forms of regression are tipped at the other end of time scale extended to the hoary past. Interestingly, both the introspectionists of modern times as well as the ancient yogis came to the same conclusion that micro-regression in retrospection simply does not work. What is interesting to note is that, after recognizing the various problems with introspection and retrospection, the ancient yogis adopted a radically different strategy: that of systematically slowing down the flow of thought *processes* rather than observing and analyzing the *contents* of consciousness. To this end, the yogis developed systematic methods of concentration: *First*, avoid switching from thoughts about one topic to those about another topic, and *second*, hold onto a particular thought for a sustained period of time. These two maneuvers are respectively called *Dhāraṇā* and *Dhyāna*, and they constitute the sixth and seventh "limbs" of the eight-fold strategy of Patañjali's Yoga. When these maneuvers are accomplished, the yogic aspirant is ready to move onto the eighth "limb" of Aṣṭāṅga Yoga, namely Samādhi. As noted, the concept of Samādhi involves a series of increasingly higher levels of consciousness. As we shall see in the next section, the yogi's backward journey begins with the process of transformation of consciousness through successive stages of Samādhi. Since there are more ways in which the process of regression can happen, we may begin to describe the first type of *prati-prasava* though successive stages of Samādhi.

Yogic *prati-prasava* ("regression") #1: Going from cognitive to trans-cognitive experience in Samādhi

In the very first level of Samādhi, called the Savitarkā Samādhi, the experience is said to be not much different from experiencing the ordinary wakeful state, except that attention is steadily focused for a sustained period of time on a particular object on which the meditator has chosen to concentrate his/her attention. In such a state, the object, the word used to denote the object, and the underlying concept are said to be fused together. In his commentary on Patañjali's aphorism 1.42, Vyāsa gives an example of what this would mean. Suppose the object of concentration is a cow, then cow as a physical *object*, and the *word* cow which denotes this object, as well as the *concept* of cow as it means to the meditator, are inseparably superimposed in the experience in the initial state of Samādhi. Although we may not see anything strange in this example, Vyāsa explains where the problem lies.

While the *animal* cow is a physical object (in a three-dimensional space, as we may put it in contemporary perspective), he points out the *word* cow pertains to a different domain involving syllables and sounds. Further, the *concept* of cow belongs to yet another domain: the domain of language, meaning, and semantics. In other words, in such a situation, three entities belonging to three different domains of reality are fused together in a rather indiscriminate way. But there is much more to this complaint about conflation of different levels involved in the cognitive process. The next higher level of Samādhi offers something much different.

In the next level of Samādhi called the Nirvitarkā Samādhi as described by Patañjali in the next aphorism (1.43), the meditator is said to leave behind everything stored in her/his memory. In his commentary on this aphorism Vācaspati explains what is dropped off from the storehouse of memories: The convention by which a word or sound *denotes* the object, as well as everything that the word *connotes* – the *meaning* of the *concept* represented by that word. This includes everything that is conveyed by that concept through the knowledge of sciences (*āgama*) known to, and understood by, the meditator as well as any and all inferences drawn by the meditator from his/her understanding of the same. Such dropping off of everything learned about a class of objects (as in the example of the cow) would indeed be a very profound change in the state of the meditator's mind. To put it in the language and idiom of Western philosophy, only whatever is "given in experience" – sensations like whiteness, qualia, and so on – would be retained, while all that is "added by the mind" is dropped off. Imagine different persons, all looking at a cow: An ordinary person interested in cow's milk; a dairy farmer, a butcher, a veterinary surgeon, or a biologist with deep knowledge of the various breeds of cows. Now imagine that all of them attaining a Nirvitarkā Samādhi and think of what each one of them will have lost. What she/he is left with is the sensorial image of the object, which according to the Sāṁkhya-Yoga theory, involves the "subtle" *tanmātra*s as distinguished from the multiple layers of verbal conventions and meanings superimposed on the sensorial base. Having withdrawn attention from the outer world of space within which the object and the body of the meditators are located, the meditator is left with the purely sensory experience. Such an experience of a person in the state of the Nirvitarkā Samādhi must necessarily have two components: *first*, an experiential or "mental" component, and *second*, a physical/physiological component grounded in the working of the sense organs of the meditator. In other words, what is involved in such an experience is a psycho-physical entity that straddles across the Cartesian divide of mind and body. Thus, the *tanmātra*s, as conceived in the Yoga system, are entities quite distinct from the frameworks based on Descartes' mind/matter dichotomy.

A little detour into developmental psychology

Here let us take a little detour into modern psychology and understand the world of Yogic meditation which may appear alien – even outlandish – to those acquainted with modern psychology. A quick look at developmental psychology would indicate how, as Piaget (1970) puts it, the first stage of development of a child is the "sensorimotor" stage in which the newborn infant "knows" the surrounding world through sensory input and approaches it through motor capacities she is equipped with – reaching out to an object, grasping, putting in the mouth, and so on. In other words, cognitive capacity starts to build on the foundation of sensory input. In a subsequent stage, the child learns about objects in her environment, such as cat and dog as house pets, various toys and so on. The mother explains how cats are different from dogs, and teaches her child object-word association: First the sound "meow" and then the sound "cat" to *denote* objects in a class. Eventually the child may recognize loyalty as a characteristic of dogs, and not of cats, which is a matter of acquisition of *connotations* of words. Eventually the little girl may become a veterinary doctor or a biologist and know a lot about the phylogenesis of animals such as cats and dogs in terms of the cutting-edge science known in her day. This implies cognitive development from a relatively simple beginning in what is given in senses to a high level of cognitive complexity.

The same thing said previously can now be said differently. The order in the development of a child's cognitive capacities involves a set of "layers" so to speak, which arise in a specific order: Sensation, object-word association, denotative meanings, connotative meanings, and complex concepts based on science. If this is correct, then what the Yogic account of going from Savitarkā Samādhi to Nirvitarkā Samādhi involves can be viewed as a "peeling off"[3] of layers of which complex cognition is composed in a *reverse order* of cognitive development. It is a process of a sort of "deconstruction" as opposed to the natural process of cognitive "construction" – implying a form of regression, yet quite different from regression in Freudian psychoanalysis.

With this little detour in cross-cultural understanding of concepts, we can return to Patañjali's view of *prati-prasava* in the next chapter.

Notes

1 *ekasamaye ca ubhayānavadhāraṇam*| Patañjali, 4.20.
2 *cittāntaradṛśye budhhibuddheratiprasaṁgaḥ smṛtisaṁkarasca*|| Patañjali, 4.21.
3 It is interesting that the metaphor of "peeling off layers" is found in a discussion of how Freud's technique was influenced by his Jewish background. Freud's technique of free association seems to have been based on the technique of "jumping and skipping" from one thought to another developed by the 13th century

Kabbalist mystic called Abraham Abulafia (see Scholem, 1941, pp. 135–136). In commenting on this historical background, J.H. Berke (2015) in his book *Hidden Freud* observes that the technique of free association allowed Freud to "*peel back layer upon layer* of disturbance, to penetrate anxiously concealed thoughts and feelings, and to initiate understanding, first in himself, then in his patients" (p. 41; emphasis added).

4 Patañjali's view of *prati-prasava*, continued

Yogic *prati-prasava* ("regression") #2: The yogi's movement from *tanmātra* of one modality to another in the reverse order of their evolution

The commentaries on Patañjali's aphorism 1.45 by Vyāsa and Vācaspati discuss the relation between the "subtle" *tanmātra*s – psycho-physical/experiential entities – grounded in sensory experience. A related discussion involves the relationship between *tanmātra*s as "molecular" parts of a whole domain. Thus, if a pot is the object of concentration, then it is a whole made of molecular units of matter. It manifests as a pot in mundane reality as a single whole entity unto itself as it is a useful object for keeping or carrying fluids. In that context, its *utility* is what constitutes the "potness" of the pot which disappears if, and when, the whole breaks into parts either as shards or molecules since such parts can no longer serve the function of containing or carrying fluids. This is a general example; we can easily think of a cat as an example instead, and view it as composed in our experiential world as being composed of shape (four legs and a tail, etc.) and color (white with black spots), touch (soft fur), sound (meow), and smell (of deodorant, maybe?). These "parts" of which the whole cat is composed are "useful" for me to cuddle, feed, clean, and variously "use" the whole as a pet. The point of all this discussion should be clear: That there is one level of reality – that of physical objects as whole made of parts – and another level of reality – which is of "real life" as we humans live, in which objects have meanings often defined by the utility of objects for our purposes. What Yogic meditation demands and offers is to transport a person from the domain of mundane reality of practical purposes to the domain of sensory experience of *tanmātra*s into which a meditator gets "transported".

According to Patañjali (1.45),[1] once a meditator becomes completely tuned in to the experiential domain of the *tanmātra*s, then she/he is said to be able to move through the hierarchy of the *tanmātra*s step-by-step from

DOI: 10.4324/9781003279860-5

gross to *fine* (See Chart 4.1). What this means is that the physical object in space is no longer the focus of attention. Rather, attention is focused on the mental content composed on sensory inputs on which the cognitive experience is based. Understood in the Sāṁkhya-Yoga terminology, this means that in the Nirvitarkā Samādhi the meditator experiences the five *tanmātra*s (elemental *psychophysical* units) of smell, taste, sight, touch, and sound, all bundled together in their cumulative form. It is important to note that at this stage, the meditator has moved away from the normal cognitive experience; there would be no awareness of the object of perception with its denotative and connotative meanings.[2] From here on, with the experience of the five-fold sensorium as base, the meditator is said to proceed to successively "finer" or more subtle *tanmātra*s, dropping one *tanmātra* at a time. In aphorism 1.45 what Patañjali tells us is that the meditator sheds *tanmātra*s in the following order: *gandha* (olfactory), *rasa* (gustatory), *rūpa* (visual), *sparśa* (tactile), and *śabda* (auditory) – which means going in the opposite direction of their creation in the course of evolution. This movement tracing back from more to less subtle *tanmātra*s is one form of *prati-prasava*.

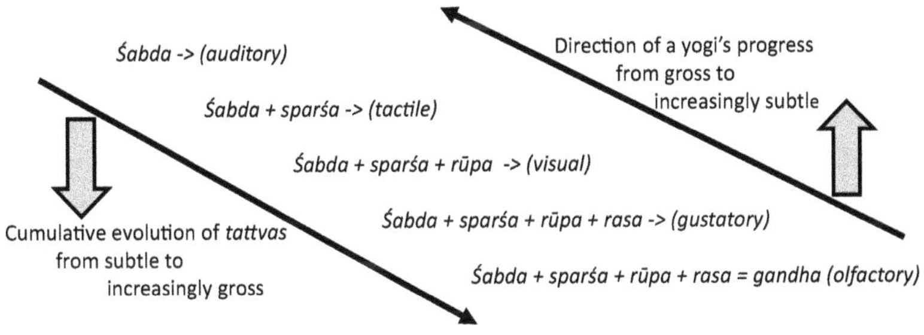

Chart 4.1 The Yogi moving in the direction OPPOSITE to the direction of the evolution of the *tattvas*

What this means, then, is that when the meditator completes the process of reversal, her/his experience would be *devoid* of sensory content, since no basis for sensory experience is left in the meditator's experience. In the context of the Piagetian model of the development of cognition, the yogi who has advanced to this stage has moved back to a stage of development prior even to birth at which a newborn is equipped with sensorimotor intelligence. From the vantage point of modern psychology, such a stage is hard to even imagine. To put it in the context of the Sāṁkya-Yoga worldview, however, this means that the meditator now goes closest to Prakṛti, the principle of materiality, which is said to be the subtlest – subtler than the domain of perceptible world accessible to the senses. The Sāṁkhya texts clarify that nothing can be as subtle as the Puruṣa, which is a step higher than even Prakṛti on the scale of subtlety. This means that there is one more move the meditator must make before experiencing Puruṣa/Self in its nascent state. The texts do point out that there are some more hurdles to be cleared before directly experiencing Puruṣa and attain *Kaivalya.* But we may leave aside a discussion about what those hurdles are and, given that the focus of this book is on *prati-prasava,* we may proceed to another example of *prati-prasava.*

But first, I may as well put on the hat of a modern psychologist once again and ask for *evidence* supporting the idea that the sensory modalities can actually be "peeled off", so to speak, and thereby empty experience of all sensory content. From the vantage point of Yoga, there is an answer to this question embedded in Yogic epistemology. As Vyāsa puts it in his commentary on Patañjali's aphorism 3.6,[3] the Yogic claims about the nature of experience at higher levels of Samādhi can be known/understood/proved by *doing* Yoga. This approach is entirely in the spirit of science. If you ask a scientist for proof of her proposition she would say: Do the experiment as I specify it, and you will get the result exactly as I have described it. Ultimately all evidence is experiential, whether the experience is cognitive or trans-cognitive. But if we are unable to replicate the specified procedure, then what do we do? We accept the word of a trustworthy scientist who has actually *done* the experiment. That means that reliable *testimony* is the next best to actually doing an experiment by one's own effort. And this is exactly what the Sāṁkhya-Yoga epistemology proposes. The *Sāṁkhya Kārikā* (stanza #4) specifies three criteria for the assessment of value of truth claims: perception/observation (*dṛṣṭa*), inference (*anumāna*), and reliable testimony of a trustworthy elder (*āpta vacana*). Thus, if we do not have our own experience of content-free consciousness, or infer it from other sources, we can rely on testimony of yogis who have successfully practiced the specified procedures and have such an experience. Thus, it should be in principle possible to verify the truth value of this form of "regression" through carefully conducted interviews of advanced yogis who may be trusted to have gone through such process of "peeling" of the layers of the sensorium. It may be difficult to find accomplished yogis and ask them what they have experienced and see if their answers tally with the textual accounts. Such an investigation is plausible and would be a research project for the future. At the time of this writing (in the third quarter of 2021) attempts are being made to launch a research project investigating first person reports of the experience of Samādhi among accomplished yogis.

Yogic *prati-prasava* ("regression") #3: retracing the stepwise evolution of the "afflictions" (*kleśas*)

Another example of *prati-prasava* or moving in a direction opposite to the direction of evolution concerns the concept of *kleśa* (commonly translated as "affliction"), generally meaning obstacles which a Yogic aspirant must remove on the path to attain *Kaivalya*. In the second chapter of the *Yoga Sūtras* Patañjali starts describing Kriyā Yoga as a means to attenuate the *kleśa*s and to thereby move on to attain the states of Samādhi. He lists the following *kleśa*s: *avidyā* (lack of correct/experiential knowledge about the Self), *asmitā* (egoism or ego-identity), *rāga* (liking/loving/approaching), *dveṣa* (dislike/hatred/avoidance), and *abhiniveśa* (clinging to life), providing brief definitions of each in aphorisms 2.5 to 2.9. Then in 2.10 he stipulates that once the *kleśa*s are attenuated, they can/should be removed through *prati-prasava*. Here we need to first clarify what Patañjali exactly means by the concept of *kleśa*.

Interestingly, neither the concept of *kleśa*, nor the five types of *kleśa*s are mentioned in the *Sāṁkhya Kārikā* and its account of the evolution of the universe. As such, for both the meaning of the term *kleśa* and for understanding the reason behind the sequence in which they may have arisen, we must look outside the *Sāṁkhya Kārikā*, focusing instead on the text of the *Yoga Sūtras* and the commentaries thereon. The basic framework of the Sāṁkhya is, of course, taken for granted, and understanding the course of evolution of Prakṛti is a must, since that is the context in which Patañajli's concepts are grounded. Indeed, we need to go even beyond the Sāṁkhya to the Upaniṣadic worldview, as some of the concepts hark back to that earlier part of the intellectual history.

Avidyā: This is the first of a series of *kleśa*s listed by Patañjali in aphorism 2.3. This is not a concept found in the *Sāṁkhya Kārikā*; it is distinctly a concept that many Upaniṣads mention, including the Īśa, Kaṭha, Chāndogya, Bṛhadāraṇyaka, and Muṇḍaka. In effect Avidyā implies the negation of Vidyā, but the nature and the relationship between them is a complex issue (see Belvalkar & Ranade, 1927). For the purpose of the present discussion the crucial point is the distinction made by the Muṇḍaka Upaniṣad between Vidyā as "higher" or transcendental (*parā*) knowledge, and Avidyā as "lower" (*aparā*) knowledge. It clarifies that while Vidyā is the knowledge of the imperishable (Puruṣa/Brahman), Avidyā is knowledge about whatever is perishable or open to change. Avidyā, therefore, involves knowledge pertaining to everything in the domain of Prakṛti. Muṇḍaka Upaniṣad explains that Avidyā includes knowledge in the fields of astronomy, grammar, as well as the Vedas – including everything under the sun, so to speak, that was known in the then existing sciences. This description should make it abundantly clear that Avidyā is *not* ignorance as the term is sometimes translated. Insofar as Vidyā pertains to the knowledge of the imperishable – Puruṣa/Brahman – it means that it is a type of "knowledge" attained in the experience of the transcendental Self in the state of pure consciousness. Avidyā, then, implies lack of that type of knowledge, but it involves all types of knowledge attained in the wakeful state through sensation, perception, cognition, and the use of reason. In other words, Avidyā includes all sciences involving the rational/empirical form of knowledge. For Patañjali working within the "Vedic" fold of the six "orthodox" systems of philosophy in the Indian tradition, this Upaniṣadic background including the difference between Vidyā and Avidyā must have been taken for granted.

But then Patañjali gives his own definition of what he means by Avidyā (in aphorism 2.5). He says that Avidyā involves mistaking the non-eternal, impure, painful, and the non-self to be eternal, pure, pleasurable, and the Self (my translation). This definition clearly pertains to how individuals perceive themselves, although his reference to the non-eternal and eternal clearly harks back to the Upaniṣadic distinction between Avidyā and Vidyā. To be specific, what Patañjali is suggesting here is that it is common for most people to think that the body, social roles, wealth, reputation – all of which are impermanent – would/should persist forever (insofar as I like the way they are now!). What Patañjali means by mistaking the impure for pure is that the body, which involves not only bones and muscles but also dirty and "impure" stuff like mucous and feces within itself, is taken to be "pure" by ignoring the odious aspects of the body. The mistaking for the painful for the pleasurable implies Patañjali's view that, in whole, there is more suffering in life than happiness (aphorism 2.15). It is common for many people to ignore suffering and think of (or keep hoping for) an ultimately pleasurable life. For if we did not think so, life would not be worth living – as the small minority of those who commit suicide seem to believe. Finally, it is the mistaking of the non-self as Self which is very crucial from the Yogic point of view. After all, the Yogic enterprise of stopping the flow of thoughts in the mind is aimed at directly experiencing Puruṣa, the transcendental Self, and thereby ending all suffering in life. To put it simply, Patañjali's view of Avidyā is essentially the same as that of the Upaniṣads, except that he translates it in terms of its implications for life as commonly lived.

Here we need to return to the focus of the present study, which is on *prati-prasava*. To that end, we need to first examine the origin of Avidyā, the ground of all other *kleśa*s, in the evolutionary order, and then see where the other *kleśa*s stand in relation to Avidyā. Otherwise, we would not be able to ascertain whether or not the enterprise of Yoga involves going against the evolutionary order. In this regard, it should be clear that the primordial Puruṣa, who is eternally in the state of pure consciousness, would by Himself never be in the state of Avidyā. Avidyā is relevant only for humans (and non-human beings) who must depend on sensory input on which to base any form of knowledge, including empirical/rational knowledge. If this is correct, then the origin of Avidyā must be traced back to the juncture when the "One" Puruṣa turned Himself into "Many" *puruṣa*s. Another way of saying pretty much the same thing is that it is when the pristine and uninvolved Puruṣa began His unseemly contact with Prakṛti that Avidyā must have made its first appearance. Presumably, that is when countless living beings or "embodied souls" (*śārīra ātmans*) came into existence and started their journeys in "*saṁsāra*" – a perpetual "run" along the chain of causes and their effects governed by the Law of Karma. That implies that the origin of Avidyā goes back to the very beginning of the evolution of Prakṛti governed by the Laws of Nature such as the Law of Karma.

Asmitā: If we look at Chart 2.1, then Mahat (the "Great One") is the first product of evolution of Prakṛti and is alternatively identified in Sāṁkhya as the *buddhi* or "intellect". This makes intuitive sense because any living being must have basic or minimum level of "intelligence" even prior to receiving sensory input. For without basic ability to *use* the sensory input, no knowledge of any form or shape would develop. Even the lowliest creature must be able to "understand" the difference between what is edible and what is not, between prey and predator. The ability to recognize such differences counts for the survival of "me", no matter how crude the "I" might be. The very next step in evolution as per the Sāṁkhya model is the ego, or the experience of *Asmitā* or "I am-ness". Here again, since neither the *Sāṁkhya Kārikā* nor the *Yoga Sūtras* say much about when, why, or how egos emerged in the course of evolution, we are left to our own means to make sense of the ideas and go from there.

In this context, I am reminded of a story from the Kaṭha Upaniṣad (2.1.1)[4] which seems to describe the "scene" of that time when the "One" Puruṣa begat "Many" *puruṣa*s. It speaks of the "Self-caused" which "pierced openings [of the senses] outward" (Radhakrishnan, 1953/1994, p. 630). This is clearly a reference to the genesis of countless living beings on earth, and their getting equipped with sensory capacities, whether primitive or advanced. I am prompted to imagine a primordial scene when forms of life began to evolve wherein there is a swarm of living creatures in a vast sea. Nature (Prakṛti) has presumably endowed each creature with some level of intelligence (*buddhi*) along with senses, which are like the mythical holes pierced through the skins that enclose their bodies, as the Kaṭha Upaniṣad suggests. I imagine, further, that being "chips of the old block" – namely the Puruṣa, their Creator – the creatures would have some form of consciousness reflected from the pure consciousness of their origin in Puruṣa. According to the Sāṁkhyan worldview, the *sattva* component of Prakṛti, which is conceived as "translucent", affords all living beings a medium that reflects the pure consciousness of the Puruṣa to the degree to which it is filtered through the senses. Yet, the living beings He begat are not infinite like Him, but independent creatures that have finite bodies and limited capacity of the senses that permits them to have some "understanding" of their vast surroundings. It is as if each living creature has independent existence of its own; each has a center of awareness stuck inside a sack of skin, with a capacity for awareness limited by the efficacy of the sense organs. (Think of the parallel development of the sensory capabilities and of the sense organs as indicated in Chart 2.1.)

With this imaginary scene built upon the story of the Kaṭha Upaniṣad, plus the story of evolution according to Sāṁkhya, we can now speculate on how *Asmitā* or a sense of "I am-ness" must be reasoned to be the immediate product of Avidyā. As finite creatures surrounded by other finite creatures, each is potential prey as well as a predator to other creatures in the vicinity – depending on the position of that creature in the food chain. As the well-known text *Śrīmad Bhāgavatam* (1.13.47) affirms, one living being is food for another (*jīvo jīvasya jīvanam*). Presumably, even as each living creature inherits a limited form of consciousness afforded by the capacity of the senses, each creature would strive for perpetual life insofar as it would reflect the eternal character of Puruṣa from which it arose. No wonder Darwin viewed all living creatures as involved in an incessant struggle for survival – implying a striving for self-perpetuation. After all, some parallels between Sāṁkhyan and Darwinian views of evolution cannot be ignored, regardless of the many differences between them! Although a Darwinian scholar may not grant anything like an "ego", let alone consciousness, to primitive living creatures, the Sāṁkhya-Yoga vision admits primitive sense of "I am-ness" along with a certain level of consciousness in all living creatures, whether primitive or evolved to any degree.

Rāga and *dveṣa*: Once we imagine the existence of countless individual creatures endowed with whatever degree of awareness (or consciousness) and intelligence and a propinquity for continued existence – or survival – then the twin tendencies of like and dislike, love or hate, must be presumed as the next most natural outcomes. For sheer survival, a living being must find nutrition in anything it can manage to ingest from the food chain. The creature must *approach* potential food and also *avoid* becoming a food item to some other creature on the upper side of the food chain. These twin tendencies of approach-avoidance, like-dislike, love-hate are universally recognized features of living beings whether non-human or human. Patañjali's terms for these twin tendencies are *rāga* and *dveṣa*. This is a fundamental binary born of the "me versus not-me" binary. The same two elements of the binary were called Eros and Thanatos respectively by Freud, and approach and avoidance by behaviorists. Call them by whatever names, these twin tendencies must be recognized as common features of all living beings. What is unique about Patañjali's view about them is that, while biologists and psychologists of most stripes consider loving and hating as natural propensities of organisms, Patañjali considers them to be *kleśa*s or "afflictions". Presumably, love and hate are "afflictions" in the sense that they are obstacles in the march to the goal of *Kaivalya*, no matter how natural and serviceable they are in organisms. The next and last item in Patañjali's list of afflictions is *abhiniveśa*, which we now need to consider before taking an overview of the list and examine Patañjali's idea of treating them to the strategy of *prati-prasava*.

Abhiniveśa: The literal meaning of this term is strong determination to attain something. In the *Yoga Sūtras* it means strong tendency to cling to life. Vyāsa (2.9) explains how all living beings, including worms and insects (*kṛmi*), tend to avoid death and try to perpetuate life. Patañjali (2.9) notes that even learned persons most intently try to cling to life, not just any ignoramus or lowly creature.

The notion of *abhiniveśa* as tendency for "clinging to life" deserves some comment. It is commonplace that most people, not just the learned, recognize rather early in life that someday they, like an old man whose death they have witnessed, must die sooner or later. The fear of dying and attempts to avoid death are of course common – except in relatively rare cases of euthanasia, suicide, and some persons who earnestly seek martyrdom. Leaving such exceptions aside, it seems to me that most people do not see death as imminent and worth worrying about, and most cope with fear of death by simply ignoring it and by getting involved in the daily grind. If this situation seems to be obvious, then why is it that Patañjali includes *abhiniveśa* as an affliction? Indeed, the other so-called "afflictions", mainly loving and hating, are fairly common – although extreme hatred for anything or anybody can be a matter of concern. Moreover, having an ego and even a sense of ego-identity (*asmitā*) are not only common, but also needed for health and well-being of persons, as psychoanalysts like Freud and Erikson would assert. What is the point, then, in Patañjali's idea that all these common – and even desirable – aspects of life are "afflictions" to be overcome?

A short and quick answer to this question is that these so-called afflictions are obstacles in the path to Self-realization. Moreover, Patañjali suggests *prati-prasava*, or a reversal in the process of the manifestation of such "afflictions" in life as a desirable course of action. Surely this idea needs a serious examination and explanation, which will follow.

The waxing and waning of the "afflictions"

Patañjali (2.4)[5] is quite clear in recognizing that the afflictions are not always present in equal force all the time; they are, now and then, either dormant or weakened, interrupted, or present in full force. This is a matter of common observation. Thus, my fear of death is most often dormant, but it may be moderately aroused if and when I hear of the death of an acquaintance younger than myself. But when I hear that a patient diagnosed of a deadly virus is just taken to the hospital from a tenement one floor up during days when the virus is rampant around the world, I may become acutely aware of my own mortality. Also, my sense of hatred for the neighboring country may become acute when border skirmishes break up and I hear that many deadly weapons are amassed at the trouble spot. However, my negative feelings for the menacing country may wax and wane with daily news of the relative success and failure of the ongoing talks between countries that raise hopes and fears on daily basis. There is no need to add examples or cite empirical data. The point to note in the context of one's own awareness of love, hate, fear of death and so on, is Patañjali's (2.10)[6] suggestion that all the "afflictions" *can be* weakened or attenuated. Given the overall emphasis on self-control in Yoga, the implication here is that the afflictions can be *voluntarily* attenuated or reduced in intensity. More specifically we may note that once weakened, the afflictions can be re-absorbed into their origin through *prati-prasava* – by going in the reverse direction of their origin. Finally, he says, that the afflictions can be fully overcome or abandoned with the help of meditation (2.11).[7] But for all this to happen, there must first be a method for the weakening of the "afflictions;" and yes, Patañjali outlines a method for accomplishing this task. *Kriyā Yoga* is the name of the method, which not only promises to attenuate the afflictions, but also prepares an aspirant for the experience of Samādhi (Patañjali, 2.2).[8]

Notes

1 *sūkṣmaviṣayatvaṁ cāliṅgaparyavasānaṁ* | (Patañjali, 1.45)

2 Once a meditator has withdrawn her/himself from the normal focus on the object of attention, then she/he would also be withdrawn from the normal context of the objects residing in a three-dimensional space (*deśa*), existing over a period of time (*kāla*), and open to causal forces (*nimitta*) – such as being moved by an impact and so on. This disconnection with the "reality" of space, time and causality is difficult to grasp as most of us take that "reality" of three-dimensional space and causality as eternal presuming that there is nothing *beyond* it. Surely, a meditator's withdrawal from the scene does not mean that objects will cease to be affected by causes. As such, when Vyāsa in his commentary on Patañjali's aphorism 1.44 suggests that a meditator in the Nirvicārā Samādhi is beyond space, time, and causality, it must mean that she/he is no longer in touch with objects in space/time as she/he was during wakeful consciousness. What this means, I think, is that experiencing Nirvicārā Samādhi implies that the meditator enters a zone of pure consciousness which is outside of the domain of space, time, and causality. Pure consciousness is clearly recognized as eternal (beyond time, past/present/future), is ubiquitous (we can tap into consciousness anywhere is space, not just on earth), and that pure consciousness, unlike in wakeful states, remains unaffected by causes – material, efficient, final or whatever. This idea about the nature of consciousness goes clearly beyond the basic assumptions of science, which

deals with space/time/causality. As such, claims to the experience of Nirvicārā Samādhi are likely to be considered "mystical" and be dismissed by those committed to the worldview of science.

3 *yogo yogena jñātavyo yogo yogātpravartate* | Vyāsa, 3.6.
4 *parāñci khāni vyatṛṇat svayaṁbhūḥ* | Kaṭha Upanisad, 2.1.1.
5 *avidyā kṣetramuttareṣāṁ prasuptatanuvicchinnodarāṇāṁ* | Patañjali, 2.4.
6 *te pratiprasavaheyāḥ sūkṣmāḥ* | Patañjali, 2.10.
7 *dhyānaheyāstadvṛttayaḥ* | Patañjali, 2.11.
8 *samādhibhāvanārthaḥ kleśatanūkaraṇārthasca* | Patañjali, 2.2.

5 Kriyā Yoga

An overview of Kriya Yoga, a three-part procedure recommended for the yogic aspirant

Kriyā Yoga involves three parts which together are aimed at attenuating the afflictions and preparing the practitioner to attain Samādhi. At the start of the Second Chapter of the *Yoga Sūtras* Patañjali lists the three parts of Kriyā Yoga:

1 *Tapas*, which basically involves practicing austerity,
2 *Svādhyāya*, meaning self-study, and
3 *Īśvara Praṇidhāna*, which involves surrendering fruits of all of one's actions at the feet of God.

Each of these parts needs short description and explanation. It may be recalled that these three are among the five aspects of observances (Niyamas) which, along with cleanliness and cultivation of contentment, together constitute the second of the eight "limbs" – the eight-fold strategy of Yoga. It is interesting that Patañjali discusses them separately in the second chapter of the *Yoga Sūtras*.

Tapas (Austerity): The term *tapas* is commonly translated as austerity or asceticism, which is common in rituals of most religious traditions. In general, *tapas* involves voluntarily denying oneself some ordinary pleasures – such as by fasting, or observing specific restrictions on eating or drinking – that most people commonly indulge in in their daily lives. The other side of asceticism is to stoically sustain unpleasant conditions such as being in cold without proper garments or suffering pangs of hunger for predetermined periods of time. There are not many examples of austerities in the major commentaries of the *Yoga Sūtras* but a couple of them are mentioned in Bhoja's commentary on Patañjali's aphorism 2.1. In those examples, a person voluntarily chooses to follow specific restrictions either on type or quantity of diet, or on

DOI: 10.4324/9781003279860-6

fasting over certain periods of time. In other words, one voluntarily denies some common pleasures in a time-ordered fashion. This is a common feature of rituals in many religions; Hinduism has many of them, called *vrat*. Fasting during daytime for entire days in the month of Ramadan is a well-known practice among Muslims. As can be easily seen, such rituals involve going counter to what one likes (e.g., delicious savories) and hates (staying hungry, getting up at ungodly hours) – and thus blunting two major "afflictions" by directly going against the demands of body and mind. Sustaining privations also involves learning self-control, implying strengthening the Ego in dealing with the impulses of the Id – to put it in Freud's language. Moreover, as far as Yoga is concerned, systematic and voluntary control of body and mind is its very essence. Vyāsa[1] declares at the beginning of his commentary of the second chapter of the *Yoga Sūtras* that it is impossible to succeed in Yoga without following austerity.

Svādhyāya (Self-study): Vyāsa mentions two forms of self-study: *First*, the chanting of sacred syllables such as AUM, and *second*, the study of literatures that explain how to practice the various methods for Self-realization – such as the yogas emphasizing knowledge (*jñāna*), devotion (*bhakti*), or volition/action (*karma*) and so on. It is clear from this explanation that Patañjali does not preach exclusive allegiance to, or superiority of, concentrative meditation (often called *Dhyāna Yoga*) which he explains. He is not simply open to other pathways to spiritual self-development, but rather recommends them. It is my impression, however, that there is more to self-study than learning about the various forms of yoga. Rather, it includes a serious self-reflection inquiring about the nature of the self. The Advaita system specifies various methods and guidelines for conducting critical self-examination, such as trying to distinguish clearly between the Seer and the Seen (*dṛg-dṛśya viveka*) or finding out what remains unchanged as opposed to what continually changes in one's self-perceptions (*nitya-anivya viveka*). It is my understanding that such exercises are involved in Patañjali's view of *Svādhyāya*.

Īśvara Praṇidhāna (Surrendering fruits of one's actions to God): The meaning of this should be quite clear: *First*, it implies agency; one can and must *initiate* thoughtful and purposeful actions. *Second*, it involves abandoning a sense of ownership of the fruits of one's actions thoughtfully undertaken by anticipating some intended results. More specifically, this part of the Kriyā Yoga clearly involves the path of devotion (*bhakti mārga*) insofar as it explicitly refers to God (Īśvara). It also involves the path of volition/action (*karma mārga*) propounded in the *Bhagavad-Gītā* since it involves surrendering the fruits of *actions*.[2] Thus, Patañjali's view of Kriya Yoga is open as well as syncretic.

Surely Kriyā Yoga puts a heavy demand on the would-be yogi, and this by way of just preparation! What all this preparation is expected to accomplish is only the weakening of the afflictions, neither overcoming nor abolishing them. But suppose a seeker goes through all the trouble she is asked to take and accomplishes the attenuation of the afflictions from Avidyā through *abhiniveśa*, then what is it that she can or should do next? Patañjali's answer is quite clear on this. He says (in aphorism 2.10) that the seeker should take on the attenuated afflictions in the reverse order in which they originated (*prati-prasava*)[3] so that they can be ultimately abandoned, allowing one to become totally free from all afflictions. Taimni (2007) explains the course of reversal as follows:

> This means that Abhiniveśa should be traced back to Rāga-Dveṣa, Rāga-Dveṣa to Asmitā, Asmitā to Avidyā, and Avidyā to Enlightenment. (p. 154)

This statement clarifies the route a person is expected to traverse in dealing with the afflicted state of affairs, going back one step at a time so as to ultimately attain enlightenment. Patañjali does provide (in 2.11) a general direction saying that the way to traverse this backward journey is through meditation (*Dhyāna*).[4] But this is only a general suggestion; it is not entirely clear as to what one should do with one's striving for perpetuation of life (*abhiniveśa*) or loving and hating (*rāga, dveṣa*) and so on. Once again Patañjali as well as his commentators leave it for us to figure out what exactly to do, how to do it, and then actually do it. Thus, one is left to one's own resources to figure out the modus operandi for meditation in this context. To that end, I would venture to suggest a possible form which such meditation could take.

Recall that one part of Kriyā Yoga involves self-study (*svādhyāya*), which should clearly mean critical self-examination, a part of the path of knowledge (*jñāna mārga*). Insofar as *prati-prasava* involves tracing the process backwards, one must start with *abhiniveśa*, which is the tail end of the series which starts with Avidyā. A critical self-examination would then mean that I must carefully examine whether I wish, explicitly or unconsciously, to perpetuate my "self" in any form or shape. It should not be enough if I write in my living will that I should not be kept alive through life support systems; that my family or doctors should be "pulling the plug" when death is imminent. Trying to preserve the body like that of ancient Egyptian the Pharaohs or a modern Lenin may be out of the question (whether as unaffordable or as unthinkable), but what about the various forms of perpetuating something about "me" and "mine" after I die? How about keeping my name and reputation alive over generations to come – by making important scientific discoveries, writing definitive books that will be read by generations, making a big donation to have *my name* put on a perpetual charitable trust, or an institute, or a tomb or a tomb stone for that matter? A desire to do something or anything so that my name is remembered by future generations implies self-love, which of course is an affliction in the chain that would come after hate or *dveṣa* in Yogic terminology. It seems to me that what is involved in the practice of *prati-prasava* is that one should abandon an urge for self-perpetuation and focus rather on discovering that in oneself that is changeless – Puruṣa or the transcendental Self. In other words, it means abandoning the sense of "me" and ownership with what is "mine" or dissolving one's identification with the ego. A high demand, indeed!

We may now continue with the ways in which one could push back *dveṣa* and *rāga* or hate and love following the yogic strategy of *prati-prasava*. We can safely assume that the concept of *dveṣa* includes a variety of negative feelings such as hate, anger, fear, malice, jealousy, and so on. Any amount of "scientific" study of the nature of such emotions in human beings in general will not do, for what is demanded in Kriyā Yoga is *self*-study. All such negative emotions are to be located within oneself. A closer examination of hate or anger would clarify that it is something I love that is threatened in any and every case of hatred or anger, whether it is my wealth, reputation, family, or country. I am jealous of somebody because my self-love demands that it is really *me* who should have what he or she has but I do not. I hate the neighboring country because I love my country and care for its territorial integrity while the neighbor's army is threatening to grab some part of my country – and so on. In other words, a close examination of negative feelings shows that they are against something that I love. Once this is recognized, then *dveṣa* gets "absorbed" into *raga* in the sense that I understand the origin of hate in self-love and I turn my attention to this origin. That is how I move *back* one step into the chain of afflictions. A different way of putting the same idea is that one should investigate *who* is it that loves or hates something or other, and *who* or *what* it may be that desires self-perpetuation.

It should be clear that the question to ask is "Who am I?" An inquiry into this question is part of many philosophical and religious traditions. In modern psychology Erik Erikson (1959, 1968) has charted the course of such a quest as it commonly manifests in lives of individuals. According to Erikson, everything with which I identify my "*self*" – *my* body, family, reputation, language, class, alma mater and *my* country and so on – constitutes what he calls a "sense" of identity. Such a "sense", he maintains, is never gained and maintained once and for all; it involves "forever to-be-revised sense of the reality of the Self within social reality" (Erikson, 1968, p. 211). For many persons, attaining and continually revising a sense of identity is a task to be accomplished naturally and without much ado while facing changes and challenges of living. However, for some young people it can become a full-fledged "identity crisis" that resembles a pathological condition. Erikson insists, however, that youthful identity crisis is a normal or "normative" condition and not a sign of pathology. It may be noted, however, that answering the question "Who am I?" as part of a spiritual quest as described in Kriya Yoga (and in the Advaita) goes far beyond the quest for psycho-social identity with which Erikson deals.

What is involved in the search for the Self in Yoga and Advaita is not simply developing a "sense" of identity, which involves revising one's images of oneself or "self-definitions" as demanded by the continually changing challenges of life. Rather, it involves finding that in oneself which makes the need for continual – and unending – revisions redundant or at least unimportant. That involves discovering that which one was, is, and always will be, which is called Puruṣa in Sāṁkhya-Yoga and the Ātman in Advaita. Erikson (1968) alludes to such a principle when he affirms that "there is in fact in each individual an 'I,' an observing center of awareness and of volition, which can transcend and must survive the psychosocial identity" (p. 135). What Erikson calls the *sense* of identity during the course of developing a *psychosocial identity* is what Patañjali calls *asmitā.* While in the Eriksonian framework a sense of identity is virtually an accomplishment of sorts, in Patañjali's Yoga it is but an affliction (*kleśa*)!

If I am supposed to proceed in my quest for the goal of *Kaivalya* through the practice of *prati-prasava* as describe in Kriya Yoga, then I must seek the roots of my urge for self-perpetuation (*abhiniveśa*), my feelings of hatred (*dveṣa*) as well as love (*rāga*) into my *sense* of psychosocial identity – which would be the last bastion to conquer on the way to *Kaivalya.* Should this challenge appear to be very difficult but still worth trying, then I must be prepared to deal with an even more difficult challenge that will follow. This is because, according to Patañjali, the next link in the chain of afflictions is Avidyā. If, as noted, Avidyā is not ignorance, but knowledge of all sciences acquired through sensory inputs (called observation) and their rational analysis, then does it make any sense at all to think of all empirical knowledge as but an obstacle? One may think of the idea of wanting to lose or shed empirical knowledge as simply absurd.

This issue deserves at least a quick answer if not an elaborate one particularly in the context of cross-cultural understanding. Empirical knowledge including the various sciences is an impediment only in the attainment of Self-realization through the experience of pure, contentless consciousness. Moreover, Yoga psychology does not ask an aspirant to *permanently* dispense with empirical or scientific knowledge; it must only be *set aside* in search of the experience of the Puruṣa/Self, which transcends objective knowledge. Here we may note how the Īśa Upaniṣad (verse 11)[5] says that we need *both* Avidyā or empirical knowledge of the perishable world, as well as Vidyā or knowledge of the imperishable Puruṣa/Brahman. While the former is useful, nay indispensable, for negotiating challenges of the continually changing world, the latter can take us to the "highest good" – *Kaivalya.* Again, empirical knowledge which has its gaze always set on the outer world is not going to be useful in Self-realization, which requires us to turn our attention away from the outer world and turn it inward. In other words, turning inward requires us to turn our backs on the outer world. It is necessary to affirm, once again, that empirical knowledge including that of science is neither denigrated nor are we asked to erase anything learned in this context from our minds; it is only to be set aside while pursuing the challenging task of controlling and stopping the ongoing stream of thoughts so as to attain the experience of Samādhi and ensure Self-realization.

Should such a maneuver appear outlandish to a person immersed in Western thought it may be mentioned that there is indeed a parallel to this idea in the recent history of Western thought. This is similar to "bracketing" or *epoche*, a maneuver which Edmund Husserl (1931/1962) asked us to adopt to enable us to reach into the inner world of consciousness. In this process, Husserl said: "*all sciences which related to this natural world* . . . fill me with wondering admiration . . . I am far from any thought of objecting to them in the least degree [but] I disconnect them all" (p. 100; emphasis original). This "disconnecting" involves temporarily suspending one's belief in the outer world as well as knowledge of the sciences which explain the nature of the objective world so that one can focus on the inner world of thoughts and mental processes. Indeed, Husserl's ideas have been compared to those of Yoga by several authors (Sinari, 1965; Puligandla, 1970; Paranjpe & Hanson, 1988).

Yogic *prati-prasava* ("regression") #4: seven steps toward the culmination of journey to self-realization[6]

After explaining the procedure for Kriya Yoga in Chapter 2 of the *Yoga Sūtras* (2.26)[7] Patañjali mentions wise discrimination[8] as the fundamental means to the radical removal of suffering. In the next aphorism (2.27)[9] he identifies seven steps[10] that a yogi would take to the culmination of the journey going back to the origin of the universe. Earlier in the same chapter (in 2.15)[11] he explains that a wise person realizes that there is a balance of suffering over pleasure in life. It is with such realization that an aspirant begins her/his journey toward Self-realization. As noted, this journey involves *prati-prasava* or returning of the individual *puruṣa* to the primordial *Puruṣa* so that the empirical self gets anchored into the transcendental Self. As noted previously, in aphorism 2.27 Vyāsa explains seven steps a yogic aspirant takes during this journey. When the aspirant recognizes that the fundamental cause of her/his suffering is the lack of understanding of the nature of the true Self, she/he takes the *first* step on the long journey to Self-realization. The *second* step is taken when, following the procedures of the Kriyā Yoga, the afflictions (*kleśa*s) are attenuated. The *third* step is negotiated after the aspirant progresses to experiencing Nirvicāra Samādhi. With this experience she/he has tasted the bliss which would manifest when all the suffering will end once and for all. At the *fourth* step, wise discrimination (*viveka khyāti*) is fully realized; there is no need to re-learn or revise the lesson.

According to Vyāsa, the first four steps (just explained) toward Self-realization require the active effort on part of the aspirant. For negotiating the subsequent three steps, we are told, the aspirant's initiative is not required; they follow naturally. These final three steps involve the yogi's release from the connection with the processes of the mind (*citta vimukti*) which had formerly defined the aspirant's self-image. More specifically, the *fifth* step involves the release of the individual from the dictates of the decision-making by the intellect. As Dasgupta explains, this happens because the yogi has abandoned all desires and has attained the highest level of dispassion (*para vairāgya*). It is only when one entertains a desire to attain something that the intellect would have to decide what needs to be done, and how. Thus, overcoming desires means that there is no ego or "me" engaged in ongoing actions to help fulfill the desires. According to Vyāsa, in the *sixth* step the three "strands" (*guṇa*s) that constitute Prakṛti "become quiescent like rocks having fallen from the top of a mountain and come to rest at the base" (translation by Larson, 2018, p. 520).

This metaphoric expression likening the process characterizing the sixth step with falling rocks is opaque and hence I may hazard an explanation. As I see it, the three *guṇa*s, namely *sattva*, *rajas*, and *tamas* involve the three elements which must cooperate to perform an action. Thus, *sattva* implies a thought, particularly a volition, which prompts a specific course of action. To supply the impetus required to carry out the actions is the function of the *rajas guṇa*, which in turn must move the normally inert limbs made of matter (*tamas*) to execute the intended action. When a person overcomes all desires, there is no need for her/him to push the body into action in service of the ego – since the ego is essentially "dissolved" with the realization of the true Self (Puruṣa) as an uninvolved witness. What this means is that a Self-realized person acts selflessly or altruistically in the interest of others. The *seventh* step, then, involves the yogi's arrival at the final destination of *prati-prasava* – the backward journey – whereby he becomes a *jīvanmukta*, meaning a person who has attained Self-realization while still alive (as distinguished from persons who may attain such a state at the cessation of life). This is the ideal state described in the Bhagavad-Gītā (2. 55–72) – of a person of steady intellect (*sthita prajña*) who is undisturbed by gains or losses and maintains undisturbed peace of mind. No matter which of the three routes to the backward journey of *prati-prasava* a yogi may take, the same destination is reached, whether it is called the *Kaivalya* or *jīvanmukti*.

Notes

1 *nātapasvino yogaḥ sidhyati* | Vyāsa, 2.1.
2 *īśvarapraṇidhānaṁ sarvakriyāṇāṁ paramagurāvarpaṇaṁ tatphalasaṁnyāso vā* | Vyāsa, 2.1.
3 *te pratiprasvaheyāḥ sūkṣmāḥ* | Patañjali, 2. 10.
4 *dhyānaheyāḥ tadvṛttayaḥ* | Patañjali, 2.11.
5 *vidyāṁ cāvidyaṁ ca yas tad vedobhayaṁ saha* | *avidyayā mṛtyuṁ tīrtvā vidyayāmṛtam aśnute* || Īśa Upaniṣad, 11.
6 I am grateful to Shri Raghu Ananthanarayanan for helping me in realizing the importance of this issue for the discussion on the Yogic view of *prati-prasava*.
7 *vivekakhyātiraviplavā hānopāyaḥ* | Patañjali, 2.26.
8 Wise discrimination is my translation of the term *vivekakhyāti*. Like many other critical expressions in Sanskrit, it is essentially untranslatable in English. Various translators present varied English words as equivalents.
9 *tasya saptadhā prāntabhūmiḥ prajñā* | Patañjali, 2.27.
10 A clear exposition of these steps in English can be found in Dasgupta's (1920/2001) *A study of Patañjali*, pp. 104-105).
11 *pariṇāmatāpasaṁskāra duhkhairguṇavṛttivirodhācca duḥkhameva sarvaṁ vivekinaḥ* | Patañjali, 2.15.

6 Looking at Freud's ideas within his cultural context and in an intercultural context

A closer look into Freud's view of regression in his cultural context

As is most well-known, Freud's worldview was firmly grounded in Darwin's view of evolution. Arlow and Brenner (1964) have traced the origins of Freud's view about regression to the biological thinking of his times. They have also charted the development of the concept of regression among Freud's followers. They point out how there were different ways in which regression was explained: genetic, systemic, instinctual, phylogenetic, and biogenetic (p. 70). Further they note that Freud had considered tracing the roots of regression to the evolutionary history of the human species. A couple of references in Freud's *Introductory Lectures* may be noted in this context. In Lecture XXII in which Freud explains his view of regression in some detail, he traces the roots of regression in the history of civilization. In this context he refers to a situation where a whole community had moved away from their traditional location to a new one, while a section of that community had stayed on in the older locality. Those who stayed back are, then, thought of as having regressed (Freud, 1920, p. 339). Freud gives another example from a phylogenetic context, citing the work he had done while working as student under Brücke's direction. In this context he refers to some findings whereby the neural structures in bodies of a variety of fish had changed to a different location in the bodies of most fish, while in some of them such structures had remained in the older location (p. 340). These examples in Freud's discussion of the nature of regression clearly show that he traced the roots of regression not only in an individual's childhood memories, but further back into the history of human civilization and even in the remote history of the evolution of species such as the fish.

Arlow and Brenner (1964) quite rightly point out how Freud's view of human nature was grounded in the biological thinking which prevailed in his time. As humans were products of millions of years of the evolution of

DOI: 10.4324/9781003279860-7

species, regression must have phylogenetic origins. Building on Arlow and Brenner's (1964) excellent overview of Freud's views of regression, Bailey (1978) presented another look at Freud's view of regression, pointing out the overall meaning the concept of phylogenetic regression had acquired in psychoanalytical literature over the years. In his view, regression implied a reduction of inhibition in flouting socially learned proscriptions and rules of etiquette. As a result of reduced inhibitions, there is a tendency toward increased aggressiveness and increased pleasure seeking. In other words, the pleasure-seeking urges of the Id are let loose, so to speak. In general, notes Bailey (1978), "phylogenetic regression occurs when emotion gains precedence over intellect" (p. 28). In other words, phylogenetic regression implies that regressive behaviors of a person involve the climbing down the ladder of civilization and return to "animal" nature.

Regardless of such negative view of regression that prevailed in psychoanalytic thinking, some rather positive views of regression had started to emerge among Freud's close associates. This is illustrated in the ideas of Sandor Ferenczi, who was one of Freud's earliest followers. In his book titled *Thalassa: A Theory of Genitality*, Ferenczi (1938/1989) spoke about "regression to the mother symbolism of earth or of water" (p. 48). In his view, humans wished for the "reestablishment of the aquatic mode of life in the form of an existence within the moist and nourishing interior of the mother's body" (p. 54). Laying in the mother's womb could hardly be a negative experience for the fetus after all! What Ferenczi's ideas indicate is that important members of the psychoanalytic movement in its early days were more than prone to trace the timeline of regression beyond early childhood which Freud emphasized. Many of Freud's contemporaries like Ferenczi were well aware of the idea that there was a parallel between phylogenesis and ontogenesis. Insofar as Freud must have been aware of the parallel between phylogenesis and ontogenesis, he may have thought that it was adequate to trace regression to patient's memories of early childhood, for this source was easily accessible within the confines of the clinic. The parallel between regression within life history, the history of the development of civilization, and the history of phylogenesis was apparently taken for granted. According to Arlow and Brenner (1964) Freud's interest in finding the roots of the human psyche in the history of phylogenesis were curbed due to the relatively limited advances in scientific knowledge concerning phylogenesis during his times (pp. 70–71).

But times have changed since Freud passed away. In the emerging field of evolutionary psychology, attempts are made to locate roots of various forms of human behavior in the long course of the evolution of species (Crawford & Krebs, 1998, 2008). As Charles Crawford explains, the main point in evolutionary psychology is to locate *distal causes* of behavior deep in the phylogenetic history of human beings as distinguished from a search for *proximate causes*, such as previous experience or environmental stimuli (Crawford, Smith, & Krebs, 1987, p. 22). Obviously, this strategy is similar to Freud's view of phylogenetic regression, except that evolutionary psychology is keen to go further back into remote history in understanding why humans behave the way they do. Now if we turn from this strategy in modern psychology to the history of Indian thought, we may be surprised to find a parallel. Note, for instance, that according to Patañjali (4. 9)[1] even as memories (*smṛti*) influence current behavior, so do instinctual drives (*vāsanā*s). Although I cannot locate examples in the literature where human behaviors are attributed to specific non-human species, it is common to hear such attributions in ordinary conversations. In ordinary conversations, if someone is found to be vindictive, he is thought to have been a snake in a former life, as snakes are believed to remember being hurt over long periods and wait for an opportunity to strike in revenge. Patañjali puts such an approach in a general statement. Thus, he notes (in aphorism 3.18)[2] that by intensely focusing attention on subliminal impressions left behind by past karma, it is possible to recognize impressions left over by experience in an earlier birth in a subhuman species.

There is of course a major difference in the worldviews of Freudian and evolutionary psychologies grounded in Darwinian biology on the one hand, and Yoga psychology on the other. Yoga psychology's belief in rebirth of the soul through a series of incarnations in a succession of species is total anathema to not only Freud, but perhaps to entire Western thought. Also, the Freudian enterprise belonged to the clinic in which patients needed help in getting their weak Ego strong enough to withstand the pressures coming from the pleasure-seeking impulses of the Id. The Yogic enterprise, however, is addressed to a different type of clientele – of persons who have honed the strength of their egos through the practice of austerity and through satisfying two other requirements, namely the cultivation of dispassion (*vairāgya*) and tireless practice (*abhyāsa*) (Patañjali, 1.12).[3]

Patañjali, who lived a couple thousand years before Darwin, could not have benefited from the latter's insights about organic evolution. It was Darwin's genius that unraveled the secret of the Finch birds changing size and shape on the Galapagos Island and showed how species can undergo changes in the course of adaptation to new environmental challenges. Benefiting from Darwin's pioneering work, his followers have shown how there is a long chain of varied forms of species extending from the simplest to most complex which has evolved across hundreds of millennia. Now evolutionary psychologists compare behavior of organisms across the long history of the evolution of species and find parallels between humans and even insects. For example, they find a similarity between the bride price modern men pay in certain communities with the way in which scorpion flies give a gift of a dead insect to lure a female to get a chance to mate with her (Thornhill & Alcock, 1983; Crawford & Krebs, 2008, p. 196).[4] Now think of how Vyāsa in his commentary on Patañjali's aphorism 2.9 suggests a parallel between learned human beings and insects (*kṛmi*) insofar as both equally strongly cling to their life and avoid death – although neither of the two have experienced the pain of dying. Granting the significant differences in the worldviews of evolutionary psychology on the one hand and Yoga psychology on the other, it will be useful to see how both systems of psychology employ a strategy of regression.

Girindrasekhar Bose's Indian response to classical psychoanalysis

Girindrasekhar Bose heard about Freud through Berkeley-Hill, a British psychiatrist working in India at the turn of the century. By that time Bose had been using hypnosis in his clinical practice. Having learned about psychanalysis through whatever publications he could lay his hand on, Bose started using free association technique in his practice as early as 1909 (Hartnack, 1990). He wrote a doctoral thesis on the psychoanalytic concept of repression and published it as a book in 1921 (Bose, 1921). He founded the Indian Psychoanalytical Society in 1922, which continues to be active today. Bose sent a copy of his book on repression to Freud, who expressed his favorable impression about it in a letter to the author. Bose was engaged in correspondence with Freud for over twenty years; their letters to each other have been published by the Indian Psychonalytical Society (1966).

A most important aspect of the historical period in which psychoanalysis was imported in India was the colonial context. During the early decades of the 20th century the British Empire was at the height of its power. Much has been written about the implications of the colonial context in which psychoanalysis was implanted in India (Hartnack, 2001, 2011; Nandy, 1995). Here I wish to stress one particular aspect of the way in which European systems of knowledge stood in relation to traditional Indian knowledge systems in the colonial context. The British East India Company initiated its educational policies in India in 1835 (a few decades before the Company accessioned the Indian territory under its control to the British Empire). At that time Thomas Babington Macaulay had remarked that "a single shelf of a good European library was worth the whole native literature of India and Arabia" (Macaulay, 1835/1972, p. 241). Given such extreme denigration of the Indian knowledge systems in colonial India, Yoga as a system of psychology stood in a state of great disadvantage in its relationship with psychoanalysis. In this context it is interesting to see how Freud was perceived in India in the colonial context. As Hartnack (1990) points out: "Bose sent him [Freud] an imaginative painting by a family friend in which Freud looked like a British colonial officer. This amused Freud; as he wrote to Lou Andreas-Salome, 'Naturally, he makes me look the complete Englishman'" (p. 943). Thus, although Freud was not an Englishman, he was *perceived* in the image of the colonizers. This implies that in the colonial context, as a European import, psychoanalysis carried with it an aura of superiority in comparison to an indigenous Indian system such as Yoga. The inculcation of a presumed superiority of European knowledge systems over those of the colonized people was part of a systematic program of colonization. In *Politics of Identity,* Peter du Preez (1980) describes such a strategy as a "con" – a kind of ideological con game in which the dominant culture tries to instill a sense of inferiority among people of a culture to help perpetuate its domination. "A con succeeds", says du Preez, "when we maneuver others into accepting an identity frame in which they are inferior to us" (p. 73). That such a con game initiated by Macaulay has been extra-ordinarily successful should be obvious; even now, some seven decades after the British rule is gone from India, most Indian universities teach Eurocentric psychology. Courses on Yoga psychology are hardly to be seen in Indian university curricula today.

What is most interesting in Bose's view of psychoanalysis is that he did not fall for the colonizer's con game. He worked exactly in the opposite direction: He tried to assimilate psychoanalysis within the worldview of the indigenous tradition of knowledge. In his Presidential Address at the Psychology Section of the Indian Philosophical Congress, Bose (1930) said:

> Indian philosophy when compared with Western systems stands on a peculiar footing. In no Western system of philosophy has the psychological material been so dominant. The outlook of the Vedanta as well as of the Samkhya system is almost purely psychological.
>
> (p. 129)

He then went on to explain the Sāṁkhya-Yoga system of psychology along with that of the Vedānta. In a long article published in the journal *Samiksa*, Bose (1948) laid out his own perspective on psychology. While adopting many features of Freudian therapeutic techniques such as free association and dream interpretation in his clinical practice, he rejected various Freudian notions such as the universality of the Oedipus Complex. Part of the objection of the Oedipal theme was based on cultural relativism in a way similar to that of the anthropologist and Bose's contemporary Bronislaw Malinowski (1927/1953), who pointed out that in matriarchal or "mother-right" societies children's reaction to their father is not as strong as in patriarchal societies like Germany where the father is the main disciplining authority. In the Bengali society where goddesses like Kālī and Tārā are more popular than masculine gods, an argument similar to that of Malinowski applies. However, Bose was not simply objecting to some specific points such as the importance of the Oedipus conflict in the process of child development. He wanted to propose a radical alternative to the Freudian model of the psyche, one that is solidly grounded in Indian philosophy (Radhakrishnan, 1999) and worldview.

Bose's model, as I understand it, was founded mainly on the monistic philosophy of the Advaita Vedānta to which he explicitly refers several times in his writings. In *Concept of Repression*, for instance, Bose (1921) says that a person who successfully follows the Vedāntic path "enjoys eternal bliss even in this miserable world" (p. 61). Then he suggests that "monists [implying persons who follow Advaita Vedānta] can become fully free from repression" (p. 63). The idea in saying this is, presumably, that in the experience of unity which the "monists" are supposed to attain, all binaries are transcended, including the binaries of conscious versus unconscious, Ego versus Id, subject versus object, and so on. Bose rejects the Freudian view of intra-psychic conflict as arising from the opposition to pleasure seeking impulses arising from instinctual drives of the Id by the Ego and the moral dictates of the Super Ego. Instead, he proposes that inner conflicts arise from mutually opposing wishes such as a wish to kill somebody versus a wish to be killed by that person. This view of an intra-psychic conflict involves a radical departure from the classical psychoanalytical model. In his paper titled the "New theory of mental life" Bose (1948) explains his worldview as a form of "panpsychic psychophysical parallelism" (p. 114). Here "panpsychism" implies that the ultimate reality is "psychic" implying consciousness as a ubiquitous and inalienable feature of reality, which is a fundamental principle of Advaita Vedānta. It is within this fundamental principle of reality that he conceives of mind-body parallelism, which avoids the problem of the interaction between mind and body – a problem which Freud also avoids mostly by ignoring it. Bose justifies this form of psycho-physical parallelism citing the Indian view of the mind as part of Prakṛti, hence manifesting materiality. Thus, both mind and body are conceived to be material in nature, which avoids the Cartesian dilemma regarding mind-body interaction.

It should be quite clear that Bose's model building is inspired by indigenous Indian tradition, particularly by the Advaita Vedānta. It is important to view his allegiance to, and enthusiasm for, an indigenous Indian worldview in the context of the Swadeshi movement against the colonial subjugation of India. As has been noted by Hartnack and others, there was a tension between two sections of the gentlefolk of Bengal – the Bhadralok.

On the one side of this divide was the greatly Anglicized and Anglophile folks while on the one other side were many who were fighting against Anglicization and the British rule. Girindrasekhar Bose and his friend Jagdis Chandra Bose, the famous botanist, were closely aligned with the anti-British group. Scholars and academics of this anti-British group had started a movement for National Education where indigenous Indian perspectives on knowledge were to be favored over imported ones. In 1909 Sri Aurobindo, a great yogi, Vedic scholar and a revolutionary, was appointed as the first Principal of the National College in Kolkata. It is in the same year that Gandhi advocated Home Rule in his book on *Hind Swaraj*. As the Swaraj movement continued, Krishna Chandra Bhattacharya (1931/1954) cautioned in a speech addressed to college students in Kolkata in 1931 that the uncritical acceptance of the superiority of the British in the sphere of ideas was far more insidious than accepting their political dominance. In his view, ignoring the distinctive intellectual legacy of India would amount to "slavery of the spirit" (K.C. Bhattacharyya, 1931/1954, p. 103), which should not be allowed to happen while trying to win political independence. It is against this backdrop that we need to understand Girindrasekhar Bose's reaction to psychoanalysis as a European import. Of course, his reaction to psychoanalysis was not an uncritical blanket rejection. Rather it involved a judicious assessment of Freudian techniques by testing them in his own practice, then incorporating what was found useful, and interpret its principles within the framework of an indigenous worldview.

But then, we may ask: Where did Bose stand in relation to regression, the basic theme of the present study? To answer this question, we must turn to his book on the *Yoga Sūtras*, which was published posthumously in a serialized form in the journal *Samiksa* (Bose, 1957). In his translation of the *Yoga Sūtras* (2.10) he explicitly uses the word regression to translate the term *prati-prasava*. I have found nothing more on this issue in Bose's writings. That is as far as it goes; we are on our own for further clarification of the relationship between the psychoanalytic view of regression and the Yogic *prati-prasava*. To put it simply, the parallel between the Freudian concept of regression and Yogic *prati-prasava* has been recognized right from the first encounter between the two systems, and this fact buttresses the thesis of the present analysis.

Before concluding this section on Girindrasekhar Bose it is necessary to make one point: that the power differential between differing perspectives on psychology cannot be ignored. Now, even after seven decades after India's Independence, the power and prestige of Euro-American perspectives is largely intact. American textbooks and journals remain the most prestigious and dominant while indigenous perspectives such as Yoga are marginalized. Regardless of the worldwide popularity of Yoga as means for fitness and health and the inroads of meditation in clinical practice, Yoga is rarely recognized as a viable approach to psychology. Such power differential is a political force that essentially denies a level field in the interaction between differing perspectives on psychology at the institutional level. I have known several instances where in universities and research institutes, Indian psychology has faced stiff resistance. However, individual scholars may choose to ignore this context and treat psychoanalysis and Yoga psychology on par. Such an approach is reflected in the work of Saradindu Banerjee who, like Bose before him within the psychoanalytical circles in Bengal, continued to view psychoanalysis and Yoga with equal respect. We shall return to his views toward the end of this book.

Notes

1 *jātideśakālavyavahitānāmapi ānantaryaṁ smṛitisaṁskārayorekarūpatvāt* | Patañjali, 4.9.
2 *saṁskārasākṣātkaraṇāt pūrvajātijñānam* | Patañjali, 3.18.
3 *abhyāsavairāgyābhyāṁ tannirodhaḥ* | Patañjali, 1.12. In this aphorism Patañjali specifies the two most important means for success in stopping the flow of thoughts, namely tireless effort (*abhyāsa*) and the cultivation of dispassion (*vairāgya*).
4 Patañjali (in 3.18: *Saṁskārasākṣātkaraṇāt pūrvajātijñānam*|) mentions that by concentrating on subliminal impressions (*saṁskāras*) in one's own mind one can know about the species in which one may have been born in the past. While trying to identify roots of behavior in past prior to birth Yoga psychology is similar to evolutionary psychology, but their strategies are radically different. While evolutionary psychology, like all natural sciences, looks only at something and anything outside oneself, the yogi looks inward into oneself. Nevertheless, when it comes to belief in reincarnation of the soul, the dialogue between Yoga psychology and modern psychology would just stop in its tracks.

7 Converging trends of thought within and across cultural traditions

Converging trends within Indian thought: Bhartṛhari and Sri Aurobindo

In my view, there is a perspective on human development within the Indian tradition which is convergent with the idea that Yoga involves a process of returning to the primeval condition of pure consciousness, although at first blush the specific notion of *prati-prasava* may not appear to be involved. The case in point is Śabda-Pūrva Yoga, ascribed to the great Indian grammarian and philosopher of language, Bhartṛhari (seventh century CE). Bhartṛhari's philosophy is complex and profound, and I cannot pretend to understand, let alone explain it in any form or shape. My understanding of Śabda-Pūrva Yoga is based on Gaurinath Sastri's (1980) book on Bhartṛhari's theory of language. In it he speaks about Śabda-Pūrva Yoga as a form of *sādhanā*, or a method for Self-realization. Sastri puts in a nutshell Bhartṛhari's view of the sequence of levels of articulation of speech in language as follows:

> According to the grammarians, there is sequence in articulation of speech (*vaikharī*), there is trace of sequence in middle discourse (*madhyamā*); but, the Eternal Verbum [*Śabda Brahman*] or *Paśyantī*, is destitute of all sequence. So, [in Śabda-Pūrva Yoga] we are to pass on from the gross to the subtle and from the subtle to the more subtle, or the subtlest where sequence is entirely eliminated.
>
> (p. 83)

Sastri explains the process further as follows:

> To be precise, *śabda-pūrva-yoga* takes us beyond the planes of *vikharī* and *madhyamā* to the plane of *Pasyantī*. The modus operandi in *śabda-pūrva-yoga* is *krama-saṁhāra*, withdrawal of sequence.
>
> (p. 83; emphasis original)

DOI: 10.4324/9781003279860-8

The word *krama-saṁhāra* is important here; it literally means a *destruction* of sequence. However, as should be clear, the destruction of sequence means *going back* from spoken language (*vaikharī*) where sentences, words, consonants, and vowels follow in a sequence, to the origin of spoken language at higher levels of thought from where spoken language emerges. At higher levels of processing thoughts, which must antecede their expression, ideas are said to appear at once in a flash – like a sudden explosion (*sphoṭa*) – such that there is no sequence of units as in spoken language. At the higher level of processing thoughts are "subtle" (*sūkṣma*) rather than "gross" (*sthūla*). It should thus be clear that in Śabda-Pūrva Yoga, the process goes from gross to subtle in a stepwise progression, ultimately leading to the highest level (*parā*) of consciousness.

This should remind us of the point in our earlier discussion of Patañjali's aphorism 1.45, where a yogi is said to go on to increasingly subtle *tanmātra*s starting from *gandha, rasa, rūpa, sparśa,* to *śabda.* In Śabda-Pūrva Yoga the reversal of sequence is essentially the same, except that it is through the stages of increasingly abstract levels of language articulation. Indeed, a similar sequence is recognized in the *Haṭha Yoga Pradīpikā* of Svātmārāma (n.d./1972) which is a foremost sourcebook for postures and other "physical" aspects of Yoga. The English translation of the 109th stanza of the fourth chapter of this work states as follows: "A Yogin in Samādhi apprehends neither smell [*gandha*], taste [*rasa*], form or colour [*rūpa*], touch [*sparśa*] or sound [*śabda*]; he does not cognize himself or others".[1] Thus, there is clearly a commonality and consistency in the three different forms of Yoga (Patañjali's Yoga, Śabda-Purva Yoga, and Haṭha Yoga) in regard to the strategy of *prati-prasava* or "regression"/involution.

We may now move to another, a relatively more recent, instance within the Indian intellectual and spiritual tradition, which is convergent with the Yogic notion of *prati-prasava.* This instance is from the writings of Sri Aurobindo, a modern Yogi and a post-Darwinian thinker. In *The Life Divine* Sri Aurobindo (1914–1919/2001) conveys his views of evolution and involution in the following words:

> Spirit is a final evolutionary emergence because it is the original involutionary element and factor. Evolution is an inverse action of the involution: what is an ultimate and last derivation in the involution is the first to appear in evolution; what was original and primal in the involution is in the evolution the last and supreme emergence.
>
> (pp. 887–888)[2]

There are good reasons why Sri Aurobindo's views may be taken seriously as confirmation of the efficacy of Yogic meditation coming from the living tradition of Yoga. It may be noted that Sri Aurobindo's spiritual development (*sādhanā*) started with the practice of Dhyāna Yoga under the guidance of his first guru Shri Vishnu Bharkar Lele. Sri Aurobindo (1972) wrote the following account of what he learned from Shri Lele in his autobiographical account in a book titled *Sri Aurobindo on himself*.

> "Sit in meditation", he [Lele] said, "but do not think, look only at your mind; you will see thoughts *coming into it*; before they can enter throw these away from your mind till your mind is capable of entire silence . . . I simply sat down and did it. In a moment my mind became silent as a windless air on a high mountain summit and then I saw one thought and then another coming in . . . I flung them away before they could enter. . . .
>
> I mention this only to emphasize that that the possibilities of the mental being are not limited . . . a progressive freedom and mastery of one's mind is perfectly within the possibilities of anyone who has the faith and the will to undertake it".
>
> (Sri Aurobindo, 1972, pp. 83–84)

The passage just quoted is a first-person statement by a highly respectable sage whose integrity is absolutely beyond question; it should stand as testimony about the efficacy of Patañjali's Yoga which asks for the cessation of the flow of thoughts in the mind to attain Self-realization. More specifically, as a 20th century author who was perfectly familiar with the Darwinian view of evolution of species, Sri Aurobindo has described his journey on the path of Dhyāna Yoga as a process of *involution* – adducing the notion of *prati-prasava*.

A converging trend in Western thought: The possibility of the influence on Freud of the Jewish mystical tradition of the Kabbalah

Freud's anti-religious views are legendary. In *Civilization and its Discontents* (1930) Freud wrote about religion as a form of "psychical infantilism" and as "mass-delusion" (p. 85). In *Future of an Illusion* (1927) he wrote about religion in a similar deprecatory vein. Given this, it would appear odd that one could try to trace the roots of some of his crucial ideas in the Jewish mystical tradition. However, in his widely publicized work David Bakan (1958/1975) pointed out the alleged connection between Freud and the Kabbalah. When he published the first edition of his book in 1958, Bakan was not quite sure if Freud had first-hand knowledge of Kabbalist writings.

In the foreword to the second edition of the book published in 1975, however, Bakan mentions how he learned from reliable sources about books on this topic in Freud's personal collection. More recently in a series of articles J.H. Berke and Stanley Schneider (Berke, 2015; Berke & Schneider, 2008; Schneider & Berke, 2000, 2008) have discussed in considerable depth the roots of Freud's thinking in his personal and family background focusing in particular on various aspects of the Kabbalah. It is neither possible for the author nor necessary to enter the complex web of the history of such ideas.

It is quite well known that Freud had a deeply ambiguous relationship between his Jewish identity on the one hand and his commitment to secular science on the other. Berke and Schneider (2008) note how "there was an overt Freud, who denigrated his [Jewish] background, and a covert Freud, who was knowledgeable of and fascinated by Jewish ideas and practices" (p. 221). Against the background of the horrors of pogroms of Russia from where Freud's ancestors migrated, and strong anti-Semitism in his native town of Vienna, it makes good sense that Freud would try to publicly disown his Jewish identity while privately preserving his Jewish roots. Moreover, Freud is known to have been afraid of opposition to psychoanalysis based on it being perceived as a Jewish enterprise, which is highlighted by his hearty welcome to Jung, a gentile, to the psychoanalytic fold. That Freud has repeatedly and overtly noted his opposition to religion and mysticism is obvious and well known. His strong commitment to the worldview of secular science left no place for either religion or mysticism. But how far and in which ways he was *covertly* committed to various elements of his Jewish background or was unconsciously influenced by the Kabbalah is a moot point. Drob (2001) seemed to have arrived at a balanced position on this issue when he says:

> The thesis that Freud was an avowed Kabbalist who intentionally disguised the Kabbalistic sources of his ideas in order to avoid their being rejected by anti-Semites seems quite far-fetched. On the other hand, it seems almost certain that Freud was exposed as a child and adolescent to Hasidic and other Jewish stories, folklore and psychological insights, and that such ideas influenced him in the very profound but general way.
>
> (p. 393)

Regardless of the ambiguity and uncertainty about the influence of the Kabbalist worldview on Freud's thought, there is an apparent transition in Freud's approach which is suggestive of a possible turn toward the Kabbalah. That is when he turned from his strong commitment to natural science to interpretive human sciences signaled by his publication of the

Interpretation of Dreams (Freud, 1900). Paul Ricoeur (1970) has argued that by focusing on the interpretation of dreams Freud radically departed from emphasis on behaviors caused by energies in neurons reflected in his *Project for a Scientific Psychology* (Freud, 1895) to the domain of understanding the meanings expressed in dreams, jokes, and in texts such as case reports.[3] Drob (2001) has shown how Talmudic rules of biblical exegesis and its methods of interpretation are echoed in Freud's *Interpretation of Dreams* (p. 402).

Thus, there are arguments both for and against the influence of Jewish mysticism on Freud's thought. For me the alleged connection between psychoanalysis and Jewish mysticism provided an incentive to explore the literature on Jewish mysticism, particularly the Kabbalah. Given the present focus on the concept of regression and the cross-cultural context of its examination, the possibility of some parallels between Jewish and Hindu thought seemed plausible. I have been forewarned that there is a long and rich history of Jewish mysticism, and further that there are many trends and differing perspectives within the tradition. It is neither possible nor necessary to try to cover the entire range of the spectrum of variations of the Kabbalah. The specific model of the Kabbalah attributed to Isaac Luria (1534–1572) has been noted by Fluegel (1902), Drob (2001), Waxman (2009) and others as having features comparable to Indian thought (particularly the Advaita perspective). More specifically, this model offers elements that are similar to the notion of regression. As such it is chosen for discussion here.

But before we start with a brief account of the tenets of the Lurianic Kabbalah it will be useful to say why the Lurianic model of the Kabbalah is appropriate in view of the focus on Freud in the present discussion. Drob (2000) explains why Lurianic background is specifically relevant for the Freud's thought: "Since the Kabbalists held that the microcosm (man) is a mirror of the macrocosm (God) the parallels between Luria and Freud were readily embodied in psychological form in the writings of the Hasidim" (p. 44). Schneider and Berke (2008) point out that

> Freud's father had grown up in a Hasidic environment in Freiberg, young Sigmund was exposed to Jewish and Hasidic ideas and customs. Both Freud's grandfather and great-grandfather on his father's side were Hasidic rabbis who originally came from the Galician town of Butchatch, a stronghold of Hasidism.
>
> (p. 131)

In an earlier paper Schneider and Berke (2000) provide historical evidence (which became available as late as in 1997) about an extended meeting

Freud is said to have had back in 1902–1903 with Rabbi Shalom Dov-Ber Schneersohn, who was a scion of a prestigious Hasidic (also spelled Chassidic) lineage of the Lubavitcher Rebbe. This indicates that Freud had closer contact with the Hasidic tradition than Bakan had recognized decades earlier. Further, the continuity of the Hasidic teachings with those of Isaac Luria has been well recognized (Scholem, 1941; Idel, 2013). All these considerations underscore the importance of viewing Freud's perspective within the context of the worldview of the Lurianic and Hasidic traditions of the Kabbalah.

Here it will be useful to take a brief overview of the basic tenets of the Lurianic Kabbalah, its cosmology, and worldview. Sanford Drob (2000) has offered a succinct overview of the Lurianic Kabbalah in his book *Symbols of the Kabbalah.* The account given follows Drob with some reference to Scholem's (1941) well-known work on Jewish mysticism. The foundational principle of the Lurianic system, Drob (2000) notes, is called *Ein-Sof*, which is the name of the Infinite Godhead, and is said to involve the "Union of being and nothingness" (p. 18). As *Ein-Sof* is all encompassing and everywhere, the only way It could have some place for the world was by "contracting" Itself, so to speak. In this process of contraction, *Adam Kadmon* (Primordial Man) spontaneously emerged. From the eyes, nose, mouth, and ears of *Adam Kadmon* emerged the *Sefirot* (Archetypes of Value and Being) including *Shekhinah* (the Feminine Principle).[4] Drob observes that the various *Sefirot*, which are like "vessels", are weak and disunited, which leads to their shattering – a condition known as "The breaking of the vessels". Further, he notes that the breaking of vessels "produces a rupture in the conjugal flow between Masculine and Feminine aspects of God" (p. 19). According to Scholem (1941), the Kellipot, or "shells", are the "forces of evil [which] existed already before the breaking of the vessels and were mixed up, so to speak, with the lights of the Sefiroth . . . or residue of *En-Sof* in primordial space" (p. 267). Drob continues his overview saying that with the breaking of the vessels "begins *Tikkum ha-Olam* (The restoration of the world), which is completed by man, who via the 'raising of the sparks' brings about the reunification of the . . . masculine and feminine principles of God" (p. 19).

Some parallels between Jewish mysticism and Indian thought

Such a condensed summary of a highly complex conceptual framework, which has evolved over centuries, is bound to be laconic and hard to understand. There is, however, some respite in making sense of such Kabbalist concepts within the context of the systems of Indian thought since such attempts are not new. As far back as in 1902 Maurice Fluegel published a study comparing the Kabbalist philosophy with that of the Advaita Vedānta. Although such comparative studies are not very common, they are nevertheless continuing through recent times (Chatterjee, 1994; Mopsik, 1994; Holdrege, 1995; Drob, 2001; Waxman, 2009). In the light of this literature, and with the support of Scholem's (1941) authoritative exposition of Jewish mysticism, a few observations can be made indicating the parallels between the concepts and the worldviews of Patañjali's Yoga and the Lurianic Kabbalah.

Given that *Ein-Sof* is the central and foundational concept of the Lurianic Kabbalah, it would be useful to start with Drob's comment previously noted that the concept of *Ein-Sof* involves the "Union of being and nothingness". This reminds us of the Nāsadīya Sūkta of the ṚgVeda, which says that at the origin of the universe there was neither being (*sat*) nor nothingness (*asat*). The parallel is too obvious to need comment. We may note further that, according to Holdrege (1995) the word *Ein-Sof* literally means "without limit" and that it "is described as the Godhead in itself, in its own absolute nature, as a formless, limitless, transcendent reality that is distinct from the relative phenomenal world" (p. 196). Such description of *Ein-Sof* makes it virtually the same as the Upaniṣadic view of the Brahman. Indeed, Fluegel (1902) has observed that *Ein-Sof* "corresponds to Brahman, All, of the Vedas" (p. 18). We may note that, when Holdrege mentions that *Ein-Sof* is transcendent reality which is "distinct from the relative phenomenal world", it implies a reference to the phenomenal world conceived as *māyā* in the Advaita system and the *Prakṛti* in Sāṁkhya-Yoga.

The Kabbalist concept of the *Adam Kadmon* (Primordial Man) is the next one which we need to note. While it seems to imply the Biblical notion of Adam as the primeval human being created by God, as a broad and abstract concept it is similar to Puruṣa, the Cosmic Man as described in the Puruṣa-Sūkta of the ṚgVeda. It does not, however, appear to be the same as the Sāṁkhya-Yoga concept of Puruṣa as the ultimate and transcendental Self. Yet we may notice an interesting parallel between the Kabbalist notion of the *Shekhinah* as the "Feminine Principle" and the notion of Prakṛti which is often equated in the Yogic lore with *Śakti* as the female principle paired with Puruṣa or *Śiva* as the male principle. Further, according to Scholem (1941), *Adam Kadmon* is the "primordial man" from whose eyes lights burst forth in multiple forms and were lodged in, as it were, in finite being which evolved in the process of creation. This vision of creation is similar to the Vedic vision whereby the One Puruṣa split itself into multiple *puruṣas*, or innumerable separate living beings to whom He imparted the essential quality of awareness. Interestingly, the Kabbalist metaphor of the *Kellipots* as "shells" or "vessels" is a reminder of the metaphor of the Kaṭha Upaniṣad which envisions how the separate individual living beings were embodied souls in whose skin holes in the form of sensory organs were poked in the process of creation. Indeed, Moshe Idel (1988) makes a reference to Kaṭha Upaniṣad (2.1.15) pointing out how the metaphor of a drop of water entering the sea becomes one with the sea, which appears in this Upaniṣad, is commonly used in old Kabbalist literature. Idel specifically mentions how Isaac of Acre (13th–14th century CE) uses essentially the same metaphor, saying how a jug of water poured into a well becomes one with the water in the well (1988, p. 67). The point is consistent with the idea of regress in that the individual self is thought to merge with the One from whom Many emerged at the start of the universe. There could be more such parallels, which are unexpected and intriguing, although, given their development in diverse cultures, one can expect approximations and no exact equivalences. The similarities and parallels between the Kabbalah and Yoga are part of a larger circle of mystical traditions worldwide as the literature on mysticism has shown (Otto, 1932; Stace, 1960; Zaehner, 1957). This larger circle and its commonalities have been known as the "perennial philosophy" (Huxley, 1945).

Perhaps the commonality comes from Neoplatonism and the influence of Plotinus (204–270 CE) whose connection with India is well known (see Harris, 1982). A most crucial feature of such traditions is that they present methodologies for spiritual uplift. In view of the present focus on the parallels between the concepts of regression in Freud and the *prati-prasava* in Yoga, it will be useful to examine the Kabbalist perspective on self-development through the process called *Tikkun*, a term often translated as restoration or repair.

The literature shows how there are highly diverse and complex modalities of *Tikkun* and their myriad interpretations. Here only selective aspects of the *Tikkun* relevant to the topic at hand can be considered. To that end, it would be useful to refer to Drob (2000) who has devoted a whole chapter of his *Symbols of the Kabbalah* to the discussion of *Tikkun*. In it he mentions that according to Zohar, which is one of the foundational works of the Kabbalah, one of the many paths to wisdom is to know one's self, or to seriously ask the question "Who am I?" (Drob, 2000, p. 373). This pathway appears to be very similar to the self-examination recommended by Patañjali as the *svādhyāya* part of Kriya Yoga. To continue with Drob's account of *Tikkun*, we may note his observation that

> according to the Lurianic scheme, man's divinely appointed task to extract (*birur*) the divine light entrapped both within the world and his own soul, and through the process of *Tikkun* (restoration) return these sparks to thcir source in the infinite God, where they can restore the unity between "male and female".
>
> (Drob, 2000, p. 44)

Here the similarity between the Kabbalist and Yogic approaches becomes quite transparent. Note that for Patañjali the task for the yogic aspirant is to recognize that he/she is in essence a chip off the old block, the infinite Puruṣa, although in the mundane context he/she is a *puruṣa* – a finite creature. The process thus involves *going back* to one's original nature from *puruṣa* to Puruṣa. Also, as noted, the Yogic lore often portrays Prakṛti as the female principle (*Śakti*) which must join in union with the male principle (*Śiva*). The Kabbalist imagery is virtually identical in this respect, given that it suggests the joining together of *Shekhinah*, the female principle of God, with *Ein-Sof*, the male principle. Referring to the comparative context we may recognize how, going back to the etymological root of the word yoga as joining together or harnessing, the enterprise of Yogic practice is (popularly) said to involve joining the individual self (*ātman*) with the Supreme Self (*paramātman*).[5] In a similar way, a follower of Hasidism is recommended to "cleave" with God, and cleaving means "stick fast to" (and not to split, which ironically is the other paradoxical meaning of the same term; see Drob, 2000, p. 406). Viewed in this way, the parallel ways of thinking in the Kabbalah and Yoga should be obvious.

Here it is necessary to focus once again on the concept of regression as going back to one's root all the way to the origin of the world in God, or more specifically God as *Ein-Sof*. Here is how Scholem (1941), the highly recognized authority of Jewish mysticism put it:

> The consensus of Kabbalistic opinion regards the mystical way to God as a *reversal of the procession* by which we have emanated from God. To know the stages of the creative process is also to know the stages of one's own return to the root of all existence. In this sense, the interpretation of Maaseh Bereshith, the esoteric doctrine of creation, has always formed one of the main preoccupations of Kabbalism.
>
> (p. 20; emphasis added)[6]

Apparently, there is no indisputable proof of the idea that Freud was directly influenced by the Jewish mystical tradition, which was an undeniable part of his family history. But there is a strange convergence between his idea of going back into a person's life history and the Kabalarian view of the desirability of reversing the process in which humans emanated from God.

Notes

1 In Sanskrit, the 109th stanza of the fourth chapter of the *Haṭha Yoga Pradīpikā* reads as follows:

na gandhaṁ na rasaṁ rūpaṁ na ca sparśaṁ na niḥsvanam |
nātmānaṁ na paraṁ vetti yogīyuktaḥ samādhinā ||

2 I am grateful to Dr. Kundan Singh for drawing my attention to Sri Aurobindo's views and their source as quoted.

3 The issue of Freud's alleged departure from causes to reasons and from natural science to hermeneutics and the human sciences is controversial. Adolf Grünbaum (1985), for instance has strongly rejected the views of Recouer and other hermeneuticists in this matter.

4 Scholem (1941, p. 229) has pointed out how complicated the history of the concept of Shekinah has been. Much caution and erudition is needed to deal with such complex topics, but I just do not have enough background to do justice to such topics.

5 It is necessary to note that in his commentary on the *Yoga Sūtra* (1.1) Vācaspati Miśra prefers the etymological root of the word *yoga* to refer to one of its etymological root *yuj* meaning the state of Samādhi, and not the other root meaning which is to join together. Nevertheless, there is a common, popular interpretation which prefers the latter meaning.

6 I am extremely grateful to Professor Doug Oman for bringing this quote to my notice.

8 Convergence, complementarity, and conclusion

It is very well known that for Freud the technique of psychoanalysis was to take regression as a process going back in one's life history – as far back as early childhood, mainly to the age of about three to five. He saw the benefits of turning back the arrow of time, and described cases like those of Little Hans, Rat Man, and so on, who, he claimed, could get rid of their phobias by recalling the events of their childhood. Such benefits of these psychoanalytic techniques have been subject to critical examination over the decades. While I have met clinical psychologists and psychiatrists who confidently affirm the benefits of Freudian techniques, especially in treating obsessive-compulsive disorders, such claims of the benefits of psychoanalysis have also met endless challenges. Yet, regardless of the assertions claiming that Freud's legacy is "dead", counterclaims about the legacy's survival keep appearing in the literature (see, e.g., Westen, 1998; Wallerstein, 2006).[1] The purpose here is not to add to that running controversy, but to examine the historical origins and the significance of the alleged benefits of reversing the trajectory of human existence. Part of the continuing debate over the relevance of Freud is a discussion of the influence of Freud's Jewish background on his views, particularly about the ways in which the Kabbalist worldview may have shaped his thinking. At any rate, the very idea about the connection between Freud and the Kabbalah led me to look closely at the literature on the issue, which then led me to the literature that compares the Kabbalist ideas with those of the Advaita. Then there is only one small step that leads to the apparent similarity between the wisdom of the idea of tracing back the roots of human existence to the genesis of the universe in whatever "it" is called, whether *Ein-Sof*, Brahman, or Puruṣa.

There is no reason to downgrade or ignore the differences between Freud on the one hand and the Kabbalah or Yoga on the other. And yet they all aim at a common goal: that of redressing human suffering. Freud found himself in circumstances where he, as a Jew in the highly antisemitic context of Vienna of his time, had to choose to be a doctor of some sort without the

DOI: 10.4324/9781003279860-9

benefit of becoming a "proper" medical practitioner. It is a testament to Freud's genius that while finding a way out of difficult circumstances, he ended up founding a novel technique of psychotherapy. As he heard the woes of individuals suffering from depression, phobia, and other forms of distress, he concluded that one thing common to such cases was the need to strengthen the Ego, often unable to balance the demands of amoral desires of the Id with the moral demands. It is in this context he took recourse to the idea of the unconscious and the conscious, and suggested that bringing desires out of the unconscious into the conscious often relieves the patient of her/his distress. Whether or not his background in the Kabbalist worldview helped him in going back on the course of human development, it is quite clear that, committed to "secular" science, Freud steadfastly resisted following mysticism of any sort, whether Jewish/Western or Hindu/Eastern, despite prompting by Rolland and Jung.

Here the differences between the "spiritual" goals of mysticism stand in sharp contrast with the medical goal of relieving pathological distress. These are the goals pursued by different types of people with differing needs. While the patients suffering from distress in mundane life need strengthening of their ego, the spiritual pursuit as in Yoga demand a strong ego as a prerequisite. Indeed, Patañjali suggests the practice of austerity (*tapas*) as a means to building a strong ego before other type of techniques such a persistent and in-depth critical self-examination (*svādhyāya*) can be undertaken. In view of the differing needs and goals of a patient and a spiritual aspirant, the strategies they must adopt are bound to be different. Thus, while for Freud's patients it was good enough to trace back the timeline up to their childhood, to the aspirants starting on the Kabbalist as well as Yogic paths, the timeline would have to stretch back to the genesis of the universe. If this reasoning is correct, then Freudian psychoanalysis would not stand in conflict either with the Kabbalah or Yoga. Rather, they all can be seen as complementary ways satisfying the differing needs of different clientele. Such a conclusion following from the foregoing discussion is not novel, indeed; it is voiced in different words by Saradindu Banerjee (1994), who followed the footsteps of Girindrasekhar Bose in comparing psychoanalysis and Yoga. It is best therefore to quote his words before ending this book.

> Underlying a multitude of differences, of both theory and practice, there lies a therapeutic thread that is common in both [psychoanalysis and Yoga]. But it must be pointed out that therapeutic similarities exist between psychoanalysis and the earlier phases of Yoga-viz., Aasana (Postures), Pratyaahaara (Bringing back), Praanaayaama (Breathing practice), and Dhaarana (Concentration). The higher stages of yoga are those for which psychoanalysis has no parallel. The repressions of

> childhood and their uprooting by psychoanalysis may equip a man to meet successfully the problems of life. The method may be sufficient for that goal. But the spiritual objective of yoga, i.e., release from the chain of existence (cyclic rebirth) is attained only by a different procedure, viz, attainment of discriminative knowledge (Viveka jnaana) that is, knowledge about the factual separation of Purusha (SELF) and Prakriti-the primordial matter.
>
> (Banerjee, 1994, p. 44)

Note

1 The fact that Wallerstein's paper appeared in a special issue of *Psychoanalytic Psychology, 23*(2) shows the relevance of Freud for the 21st century. More recently, John Horgan, who writes a popular blog in the *Scientific American* magazine, discussed the contemporary relevance of Freud as recently as in 2017 and again in 2019.

Glossary of Sanskrit terms

(**Caution**: Many of the Sanskrit terms are not translatable in English terms. Only approximations are used for the sake of convenience. This is specifically true about Sanskrit terms used in the traditional literature on Yoga, where they are technical terms with specific meanings.)

Abhiniveśa: Clinging to life
Abhyāsa: Tireless practice
Ahimsā: Avoiding injury
Ākāśa: One of the five gross elements according to the Sāṁkhya system, commonly translated as space or ether
Āpa: Literally, water, but according to the Sāṁkhya system it is one of the five gross elements
Āsana: Generally, posture, but for Patañjali it implies only as a steady and comfortable posture
Asmitā: Egoism or ego-identity
Asteya: Avoiding stealing
Avidyā: Lack of correct/experiential knowledge about the Self. It also implies all forms of empirical knowledge grounded in sensation and reason
Dhārṇā: Restricting the range of attention or concentration
Dhyāna: Sustaining attention for a length of time, or contemplation
Draṣṭā: The Self as Seer
Dveṣa: Commonly it means hatred, but it may include a variety of negative feelings such as hate, anger, fear, malice, jealousy
Guṇa: Any of the three continually interacting constituents or "strands" of Prakṛti that together account for all the changes in the objective world. The three *guṇa*s are *sattva, rajas,* and *tamas*
Kaivalya: According to Sāṁkhya and Yoga, it is the highest state attainable by "isolating" the Self-as-Seer from everything open to observation
Kleśa: Commonly translated as affliction, but for Patañjali it means various obstacles which Yogic aspirants can/should remove on the path to attain *Kaivalya*

Nāsadīya Sūkta: A hymn of the ṚgVeda which speculates about the beginning of the universe

Nirvitarkā Samādhi: A higher state of consciousness in which the meditator is said to leave behind everything stored in her/his memory

Niyama: A set of observances, such as cleanliness, cultivation of a sense of contentment, etc.

Prakṛti: Principle of materiality, being one of the two ontological categories according to the Sāṁkhya system

Prāṇāyāma: Approximately speaking, breath control

Prati-prasava: Literally it means going in a counter order. In Patañjali's Yoga the term coveys the idea that spiritual development requires a person to go back to the nascent state of Puruṣa, or the One Self from which all individual beings evolved starting from the beginning of the universe

Pratyāhāra: Withdrawing of attention from objects of the senses

Pṛthvī: One of the five gross elements according to the Sāṁkhya system. While the common translation of this term as "earth" is literally correct, it is misleading, since in Sāṁkhya it means more like matter or mass, and not like the planet earth

Puruṣa: The one Self, as well as many selves, and one of the two ontological categories according to the Sāṁkhya system characterized mainly by sentience

Rāga: Liking/loving/approaching

Rajas: One of the three "strands" of Prakṛti which is roughly equivalent to "energy"

Samādhi: A graded series of increasingly higher states of consciousness

Sattva: One of the three "strands" of Prakṛti which accounts for its "intelligent" stuff

Savitarkā Samādhi: The very first level of Samādhi, or a state of concentration, in which the object of concentration, the word representing it, and the meaning of the word are superimposed or conflated

Svādhyāya: Generally, self-study; more specifically, deep inquiry into selfhood leading to the discovery of the true Self

Tamas: One of the three "strands" of Prakṛti which is roughly equivalent to "mass"

Tapas: Asceticism; practice of austerities

Tattva: According to the Sāṁkhya system, there are five *tattva*s, psychophysical elemental principles corresponding to the five senses. They are said to be psychological as well as cosmic phenomena

Teja: One of the five gross elements according to the Sāṁkhya system. The term is untranslatable in English; its common translation as fire is inaccurate

Vairāgya: cultivation of dispassion

Vāyu: One of the five gross elements according to the Sāṁkhya system. While the common translation of this term as wind or air is literally correct, it does not accurately convey its technical meaning

Yama: A set of behavioral restraints such as non-violence, avoidance of telling lies, etc.

References

Arjunwadkar, K. S. (2006). *Yogasūtras of Patañjali with Bhāṣya of Vyāsa commented upon by Vācasptai-miśra, and with commentary of Nāgoji-bhaṭṭa*. Pune: Bhandarkar Oriental Research Institute.

Arlow, A. J., & Brenner, C. (1964). *Psychoanalytic concepts and the structural theory*. New York: International Universities Press.

Bailey, K. G. (1978). The concept of phylogenetic regression. *Journal of the American Academy of Psychoanalysis*, *6*(1), 5–35.

Bakan, D. (1954). A reconsideration of the problem of introspection. *Psychological Bulletin*, *51*(2), 105–118.

Bakan, D. (1975). *Sigmund Freud and the Jewish mystical tradition* (Paperback, Ed.). Boston, MA: Beacon Press (First published 1958).

Banerjee, S. (1994). Yoga and psychoanalysis. *Samiksa*, *48*(1–2), 24–48.

Belvalkar, S. K., & Ranade, R. D. (1927). *History of Indian philosophy, volume 2: Creative period*. Pune: Bilvakuñja.

Berke, J. H. (2015). *The hidden Freud: His Hasidic roots*. London: Karnac.

Berke, J. H., & Schneider, S. (2008). *Centers of power: The convergence of psychoanalysis and Kabbalah*. New York: Jason Aronson.

Bhattacharya, R. S. (1976). Are yogangas to be practiced successively? *Journal of the Yoga Institute*, *21*(12), 179–181.

Bhattacharyya, K. C. (1954). Swaraj in ideas. *Visvabharati Quarterly*, *20*, 103–114 (Original lecture delivered in 1931).

Boring, E. G. (1953). A history of introspection. *Psychological Bulletin*, *50*, 169–189.

Bose, G. (1921). *Concept of repression*. Calcutta: Bangiya Kala Kendra, and London: Kegan Paul, Trench, Trubner.

Bose, G. (1930). The psychological outlook in Hindu philosophy. *Indian Journal of Psychology*, *5*(3–4), 119–146.

Bose, G. (1948). A new theory of mental life. *Samiksa*, *2*(2), 108–205.

Bose, G. (1957). The yoga sutras. *Samkhya*, *11*(1–4).

Brown, R. (1965). *Social psychology*. New York: Free Press.

Chatterjee, M. (1994). Rabbi Abraham Isaac Kook and Sri Aurobindo: Toward a comparison. In H. Goodman (Ed.), *Between Jerusalem and Benares: Comparative studies in Judaism and Hinduism* (pp. 243–266). New York: State University of New York Press.

Cramer, H., Lauche, R., & Dobos, G. (2014). Characteristics of randomized controlled trials of yoga: A bibliometric analysis. *Complementary and Alternative Medicine*, *14*, 328.

Crawford, C. B., & Krebs, D. (Eds.). (1998). *Handbook of evolutionary psychology: Ideas, issues, and applications*. Mahwah, NJ: Lawrence Erlbaum Associates.

Crawford, C. B., & Krebs, D. (Eds.). (2008). *Foundations of evolutionary psychology*. New York: Lawrence Erlbaum Associates.

Crawford, C. B., Smith, M., & Krebs, D. (Eds.). (1987). *Sociobiology and psychology: Ideas, issues, and applications*. Hillsdale, NJ: Laurence Erlbaum.

Dasgupta, S. N. (1973). *Yoga as philosophy and religion*. Delhi: Motilal Banarsidass (First published 1924).

Dasgupta, S. N. (1975). *A history of Indian philosophy* (Indian ed., Vols. 1–5). Delhi: Motilal Banarsidass (First published 1922).

Dasgupta, S. N. (2001). *A study of Patañjali*. Delhi: Indian Council of Philosophical Research (First published 1920).

de Michelis, E. (2007). A preliminary survey of modern yoga studies. *Asian Medicine*, *3*(1), 1–19.

Dobson, J. (1983). *Advaita Vedanta and modern science*. Chicago: Vivekananda Vedanta Society (First published 1979).

Drob, S. L. (2000). *Symbols of the Kabbalah: Philosophical and psychological perspectives*. Jerusalem: Jason Aronson.

Drob, S. L. (2001). *Kabbalistic Metaphors: Jewish mystical ideas in ancient and modern thought*. Jerusalem: Jason Aronson.

du Preez, P. (1980). *The politics of identity*. Oxford: Basil Blackwell.

Duquette, J. (2010). *Towards a philosophical reconstruction of the dialogue between modern physics and Advaita Vedānta: An inquiry into the concepts of ākāśa, vacuum and reality* (Doctoral Dissertation). Université de Montréal.

Erikson, E. H. (1959). Identity and the life cycle. *Psychological Issues*, *1*(1).

Erikson, E. H. (1964). *Insight and responsibility*. New York: W.W. Norton.

Erikson, E. H. (1968). *Identity, youth and crisis*. New York: W.W. Norton.

Ferenczi, S. (1989). *Thalassa: A theory of genitality*. New York: Karnac (First published 1938).

Fluegel, M. (1902). *Philosophy, Qabbala and Vedanta*. Baltimore, MD: H. Fluegel.

Freud, S. (1895). Project for a scientific psychology. In J. Strachey (Ed.), *The standard edition of the complete psychological works of Sigmund Freud* (Vol. 1, pp. 281–397). London: Hogarth.

Freud, S. (1900). The interpretation of dreams. In J. Strachey (Ed.), *The standard edition of the complete psychological works of Sigmund Freud* (Vol. 4, pp. 1–626). London: Hogarth.

Freud, S. (1909). [For the case of Little Hans]. Analysis of a phobia in a five-year-old boy. In J. Strachey (Ed.), *The standard edition of the complete psychological works of Sigmund Freud* (Vol. 10, Two case histories, pp. 5–149). London: Hogarth.

Freud, S. (1918 [1914]). [For the case of Wolf Man]. An infantile neurosis and other works. In J. Strachey (Ed.), *Standard edition of the complete psychological works of Sigmund Freud* (Vol. 17, pp. 3–122). London: Hogarth.

Freud, S. (1920). Introductory lectures on psychoanalysis. In J. Strachey (Ed.), *The standard edition of the complete psychological works of Sigmund Freud* (Vol. 16, pp. 243–496). London: Hogarth.

Freud, S. (1922). Beyond the pleasure principle. In J. Strachey (Ed.), *The standard edition of the complete psychological works of Sigmund Freud* (Vol. 18, pp. 7–64). London: Hogarth.

Freud, S. (1923). Ego and the id. In J. Strachey (Ed.), *Standard edition of the complete psychological works of Sigmund Freud* (Vol. 19, pp. 12–66). London: Hogarth.

Freud, S. (1927). The future of an illusion. In J. Strachey (Ed.), *The standard edition of the complete psychological works of Sigmund Freud* (Vol. 21, pp. 1–56). London: Hogarth.

Freud, S. (1930). Civilization and its discontents. In J. Strachey (Ed.), *The standard edition of the complete psychological works of Sigmund Freud* (Vol. 21, pp 57–146). London: Hogarth.

Grünbaum, A. (1985). *The foundations of psychoanalysis*. Berkeley, CA: University of California Press.

Harris, R. B. (Ed.). (1982). *Neoplatonism and Indian thought*. Norfolk, VA: International Society for Neoplatonic Studies.

Hartmann, H., Kris, E., & Loewenstein, R. M. (1946). Comments on the formation of psychic structure. *Psychoanalytic Study of the Child, 2*, 11–38.

Hartnack, C. (1990). Vishnu on Freud's desk: Psychoanalysis in colonial India. *Social Research, 57*(4), 922–949.

Hartnack, C. (2001). *Psychoanalysis in colonial India*. New Delhi: Oxford University Press.

Hartnack, C. (2011). Colonial dominions and the psychoanalytic couch: Synergies of Freudian Theory with Bengali Hindu thought and practices in British India (pp. 97–111). In W. Anderson, D. Jenson, & R. C. Keller (Eds.), *Unconscious dominions: Psychoanalysis, colonial trauma, and global sovereignties*. Durham, NC: Duke University Press.

Hiriyanna, M. (1995). *Essentials of Indian philosophy*. Delhi: Motilal Banarsidass (First published 1948).

Holdrege, B. A. (1995). *Veda and Torah: Transcending the textuality of scripture*. New York: State University of New York Press.

Husserl, E. (1962). *Ideas: General introduction to phenomenology* (W. R. Boyce-Gibson, Trans.). New York: Collier Books (First published 1931).

Huxley, A. (1945). *Perennial philosophy*. New York: Harper & Brothers.

Idel, M. (1988). *Kabbalah: New perspectives*. London: Yale University Press.

Idel, M. (2013). The Tsadik and his soul's sparks: From Kabbalah to Hasidism. *The Jewish Quarterly Review, 103*(2), 196–240.

Indian Psychoanalytical Society. (1966). *The beginnings of psychoanalysis in India: Bose-Freud correspondence*. Calcutta: Indian Psychoanalytical Society.

Īśvarakṛṣṇa. (1940). *Sānkhya Kārikā of mahāmuni Śrī Īśvarakṛṣṇa with the commentary Sārasubodhinī of Paṇḍit Śivanārāyaṇa Śastrī with Sānkhya Tattvakaumudī of Vācaspati Miśra*. Bombay: Pāṇḍurang Jāwaji (Date of composition of the *Sānkhya Kārikā* unknown).

James, W. (1983). *Principles of psychology*. Cambridge, MA: Harvard University Press (First published 1890).

Kant, I. (1966). *Critique of pure reason* (F. Max Müller, Trans.). Garden City, NY: Doubleday (First published 1781).

Kris, E. (1950). The development of ego psychology. *Samiksa*, *5*(3), 153–168 (The copy of this paper I found in the archives of *Samiksa* was incomplete).

Kris, E. (1952). *Psychoanalytic explorations in art*. New York: International Universities Press.

Krusche, H., & Desikachar, T. K. V. (2014). *Freud and yoga: Two philosophies of mind compared*. New York: Farrar, Straus and Giroux.

Larson, G. J. (2018). *Classical yoga philosophy and the legacy of sāṁkhya*. Delhi: Motilal Banarsidass.

Larson, G. J., & Bhattacharya, R. S. (Eds.). (2006). Sāṁkhya: A dualist tradition in Indian philosophy. In *Encyclopedia of Indian philosophies* (Vol. 4). New Delhi: Motilal Banarsidass (First published 1987).

Liberman, K. (2008). The reflexivity of the authenticity of Hatha yoga. In B. Diken & C. B. Laustsen (Eds.), *Yoga in the modern world: Contemporary perspectives* (pp. 100–116). New York: Routledge.

Locke, J. (1959). *An essay concerning human understanding* (2 Vols., A. C. Fraser, Ed.). New York: Dover (First published 1690).

Macaulay, T. B. (1972). Minute on Indian education. In T. B. Macaulay (Ed.), *Selected writings* (J. Clive & T. Pinney, Eds., pp. 237–251). Chicago: University of Chicago Press (Original "Minute" presented in 1835).

Malinowski, B. (1953). *Sex and repression in savage society*. London: Routledge & Kegan Paul (First published 1927).

Mopsik, C. (1994). Union and unity in the Kabbala. In H. Goodman (Ed.), *Between Jerusalem and Benares: Comparative studies in Judaism and Hinduism* (pp. 223–242). New York: State University of New York Press.

Nandy, A. (1995). *The savage Freud and other essays on possible and retrievable selves*. Delhi: Oxford University Press.

Otto, R. (1932). *Mysticism East and West: A comparative analysis of the nature of mysticism*. New York: Macmillan.

Paranjpe, A. C. (1983). Mind and minding: Some Eastern and Western views. In A. J. Krakowski & C. P. Kimball (Eds.), *Psychosomatic medicine: Theoretical, clinical and transcultural aspects* (pp. 379–388). New York: Plenum.

Paranjpe, A. C. (1998). *Self and identity in modern psychology and Indian thought*. New York: Plenum.

Paranjpe, A. C., & Hanson, R. K. (1988). On dealing with the stream of consciousness: A comparison of Husserl and yoga. In A. C. Paranjpe, D. Y. F. Ho, & R. W. Rieber (Eds.), *Asian contributions to psychology* (pp. 215–231). New York: Praeger.

Parrott, R. J. (1986). The problem of the Sāṁkhya tattvas as both cosmic and psychological phenomena. *Journal of Indian Philosophy*, *14*, 55–77.

Patañjali. (2006). Pātañjala yoga sūtrāṇi. In K. S. Arjunwadkar (Ed.), *Yogasūtras of Patañjali with Bhāṣya of Vyāsa commented upon by Vācasptai-miśra, and with commentary of Nāgoji-bhaṭṭa*. Pune: Bhandarkar Oriental Research Institute (The date of the composition of the original text unknown).

Piaget, J. (1970). Piaget's theory (G. Gellerier & J. Langer, Trans.). In P. H. Mussen (Ed.), *Carmichael's manual of child psychology* (3rd ed., pp. 703–732). New York: Wiley.

Puligandla, R. (1970). Phenomenological reduction and yogic meditation. *Philosophy East and West*, *20*, 19–33.

Radhakrishnan, S. (1994). *The principal upaniṣads*. New Delhi: HarperCollins (India) (First published, 1953).

Radhakrishnan, S. (1999). *Indian philosophy* (Vol. 2). New Delhi: Oxford India Paperbacks (First published 1923).

Rapaport, D. (1959). A historical survey of psychoanalytical ego psychology. In E. H. Erikson, Identity and the life cycle. *Psychological Issues, Monograph 1*, *1*(1) (pp. 5–17).

Ricoeur, P. (1970). *Freud and philosophy*. New Haven, CT: Yale University Press.

Rukmani, T. S. (1980–1989). *Yogavārttika of Vijñānabhikṣu* (4 vols.). New Delhi: Munshiram Manoharlal.

Sastri, G. (1980). *A study in the dialectics of sphoṭa* (Revised New ed.). Delhi: Motilal Banarsidass.

Schitz, O. A. H. (1923). *Psychoanalyse und yoga*. Darmstatd, Germany: Otto Reichl Verlag.

Schneider, S., & Berke, J. H. (2000). Sigmund Freud and the Lubawitcher Rebbe. *Psychoanalytic Review*, *87*(1), 39–59.

Schneider, S., & Berke, J. H. (2008). He oceanic feeling, mysticism and Kabbalah: Freud's historical roots. *Psychoanalytic Review*, *95*(1), 131–156.

Scholem, G. (1941). *Major trends in Jewish mysticism* (Rev. ed.). New York: Schocken Books.

Sinari, R. (1965). The method of phenomenological reduction and yoga. *Philosophy East and West*, *15*, 217–228.

Sri Aurobindo. (1972). *Sri Aurobindo on himself*. Pondicherry: Sri Aurobindo Ashram.

Sri Aurobindo. (2001). *The life divine* (6th ed.). Pondicherry: Sri Auribindo Ashram (First published 1914-1919).

Stace, W. T. (1960). *Mysticism and philosophy*. Philadelphia: J.B. Lippincott.

Svātmārāma. (1972). *Haṭha Yoga Pradīpikā of Svātmārāma*. Adyar, Madras: The Adyara Library and Research Center (The date of the original text unknown).

Taimni, I. K. (2007). *The science of yoga* (1st ed., 11th Printing). Adyar, Chennai: Theosophical Publishing House.

Thornhill, R., & Alcock, J. (1983). *The evolution of insect mating systems*. Cambridge, MA: Harvard University Press.

Wallerstein, R. S. (2006). The relevance of Freud's psychoanalysis in the 21st century: Its science and its research. *Psychoanalytic Psychology*, *23*(2), 302–326.

Watson, J. B. (1913). Psychology as the behaviorist views it. *Psychological Review*, *20*, 158–177.

Waxman, R. (2009). *Correspondences in Jewish mysticism/Kabbalah and Hindu mysticism/Vedanta-Advaita* (Thesis Master's Degree). Advisor: Skidmore College. https://doi.org/10.13140/RG.2.2.27837.10729

Westen, D. (1998). The scientific legacy of Sigmund Freud: Toward a psychodynamically informed psychological science. *Psychological Bulletin*, *124*(3), 333–371.

Zaehner, R. C. (1957). *Mysticism: Sacred and profane*. Oxford: Oxford University Press.

Index

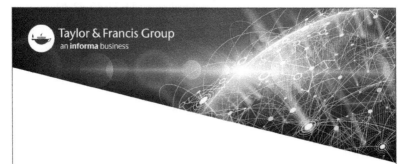

www.ingramcontent.com/pod-product-compliance
Ingram Content Group UK Ltd.
Pitfield, Milton Keynes, MK11 3LW, UK
UKHW020426010325
455677UK00029B/1021